CAVALLINO RAMPANTE

CAVALLINO RAMPANTE

How Ferrari mastered modern-day Formula 1

Nick Garton

Haynes Publishing

'I loved you, so I drew these tides of men into my hands and wrote my will across the sky in stars . . .'
T. E. Lawrence, *The Seven Pillars of Wisdom*

To my family . . . for waiting!

First published in November 2003

A catalogue record for this book is available from the British Library

ISBN 1 84425 023 7

Library of Congress catalog card no. 2003110428

Haynes North America Inc., 861 Lawrence Drive, Newbury Park, California 91320, USA.

Published by Haynes Publishing, Sparkford, Yeovil, Somerset BA22 7JJ, UK.
Tel: 01963 442030 Fax: 01963 440001
Int. tel: +44 1963 442030 Int. fax: +44 1963 440001
E-mail: sales@haynes.co.uk
Web site: www.haynes.co.uk

Designed by Simon Larkin, Haynes Publishing
Page layout by James Robertson, Haynes Publishing
Edited by Quentin Spurring
Printed and bound in Britain by
J. H. Haynes & Co. Ltd, Sparkford

Title page photo courtesy of Ferrari

CONTENTS

INTRODUCTION

In 1993, Jean Todt courageously took the reins of the *Cavallino Rampante* – the 'Prancing Horse' – and assumed the responsibility for all that it symbolised to the world. A daunting prospect to its leader even in its heyday, this was, it's easy to forget, a truly epic undertaking, as the once-great Scuderia Ferrari had found itself far from the pace of modern Formula One, and in internal disarray.

Ferrari's hold on people's imagination is the legacy of its founder, Enzo Ferrari. His magnetic charisma was the catalyst that brought the most idolised sportsmen in their field to his stronghold in Maranello and placed them in the Scuderia's evocative scarlet racing cars. He created a legend and all the expectations that legendary status brings, and it was Todt's inheritance to live up to those expectations amid all the pandemonium they create.

Between 1993 and 1995, Scuderia Ferrari was rebuilt from within. Rifts were healed, the foundations for new structures were laid and a sense of unity hammered relentlessly into place. In 1996, the team gained the incomparable services of double World Champion Michael Schumacher and the resources of Shell in developing the strength and reliability of its cars.

Then, in 1997, Ferrari was reborn as Scuderia Ferrari Marlboro, and lavish funds resulted in a new, brighter shade of red enveloping the cars of Rory Byrne and the team directed by Ross Brawn. This definitive team fought its way towards domination through ferocious and often-controversial showdowns with the Williams and McLaren teams, riding the storms of public hysteria they brought about. Disappointment followed disappointment but then, in 2000, the pendulum swung and the Scuderia entered an era of total supremacy.

The long years of rebuilding, conducted by Jean Todt, brought together a team better able than any other to explore and exploit every thought and idea. In Michael Schumacher they gathered around a man who has simply stood alone as a racing driver in terms of consistency, determination, focus and sheer speed for season after relentless season. Together they swept to one side any semblance of opposition and set about the task of making history.

Here is an account of how those years of domination have been created and executed. Looking exclusively behind-the-scenes of the fabled Gestione Sportiva, every component of the world's most famous racing team and its success is revealed, to show how Ferrari once again became the team against which all others must be judged.

The team's key personalities describe the scale of the challenges that were presented to them and how those challenges were overcome. The team members and technical partners who engineered this greatest 'Ferrari era' provide unique insights into their day-to-day lives and are given the chance to answer their many detractors.

Uniquely amongst the greatest teams in Grand Prix history, the gulf in performance between Ferrari and their rivals has brought as much condemnation as applause. In the days of Juan Manuel Fangio or Ayrton Senna the sheer prowess of a great team brought people to Grands Prix simply to witness their brilliance, yet that sits uneasily with today's stylised ideal of sport as a thrilling contest of equals. It is a myth that is no more valid in football or athletics than it is in Formula One, yet the display of intolerance shown towards Ferrari's successes by the media and the public is without precedent. To the Gestione Sportiva it is just another hurdle for the team to overcome, but it has often made for an unedifying spectacle.

In reality empires rise and fall under their own momentum. Already the shadows are lengthening on the era of Scuderia Ferrari Marlboro and Michael Schumacher, but as yet there is still no challenger whose brilliance is as consistent or whose determination is as unwavering.

We should enjoy it while it lasts, just as surely as we should salute the new champions as and when they emerge. One day the headlines will again ask when Ferrari will ever fight its way back into contention, and the hysteria will gather pace behind a new Scuderia Ferrari with a new star in its midst. The successors will, however, face a considerable challenge in getting anywhere close to the achievements of Michael Schumacher and the rest of Jean Todt's team.

This is the story of how they did it...

Opposite: Job done! Rubens Barrichello, Ross Brawn, Jean Todt and Michael Schumacher celebrate another record-breaking day for the Cavallino Rampante at Suzuka in 2003. (Ferrari)

ACKNOWLEDGEMENTS

Motor sport in every facet – even writing about it – is a team effort. It is with the deepest thanks to Luca Colajanni and Regine Rettner of the Scuderia Ferrari Marlboro press office that this book has happened at all, and also to Peter Secchi of PRISM who has represented Shell's tremendous input to this book.

For their time and hospitality when I visited Maranello, and for their insights into making the most formidable team in world sport bar none, those same thanks must be extended to the whole Gestione Sportiva, who wrote this story.

Equally, thanks to Agnes Carlier and the Sauber Petronas team, Mike Copson at Shell and Rachel Ingham at Bridgestone, without whom Ferrari would struggle to compete, and I would have struggled to complete the picture of life at the top.

Personally, I would like to thank Jonathan Gill, Matthew Carter, Deborah Tee, Alan Gow, Eilish O'Shea, Juliet Edwards, Richard Rodgers, Lyn StJohn, Steve Madincea, Bob Lobell, Eve Wheeler, Joe Saward, Alan Henry, David Tremayne and the late Bruce Hepburn and Derek Wright for the belief they have shown in me over the years.

Most of all thanks to Mark Hughes, Steve Rendle, Quentin Spurring and all at Haynes for their dedication to seeing this project through.

Chapter One

'IN BOCCA AL LUPO'

In a world that is almost always becoming – almost never being – it's easy to forget where you are. Sometimes it's easy to forget who you are. For the multi-billion dollar circus that is Formula One, moving on is how everyone feels most at home.

There is one exception to this strange existence. It comes each September, as Formula One prepares to bid farewell to its European base for another year, and the circus takes up residence in the Villa Reale parco at Monza, half an hour's drive from Milan. This is the moment when Grand Prix racing is confronted by its roots, when the studied indifference of the paddock is overwhelmed by the Gran Premio d'Italia.

The first pickaxe bit into this old royal park in February 1922, at the hand of Felice Nazzaro, Italy's first Grand Prix winner. It took seven months, 3,500 labourers, 200 horses and carts, 30 lorries, and a narrow-gauge railway to complete the construction just a week before the first Gran Premio – a race that would come to define an age when the world was ruled by poets, passion and danger.

The opening lines of an official guide to the Autodromo Nazionale di Monza encapsulate the relationship between Grand Prix racing and its Italian home. 'Speed is a charming and ruthless goddess who often demands human sacrifice in exchange for the ecstasy she offers,' it says. 'Her most famous temple is, perhaps, Monza, where exhilarating speed rites have been, and continue to be, celebrated on the track winding its way under the trees in the park.'

Into the wolf's mouth: Michael Schumacher walks out to try and rescue the World Championship for Ferrari at the fifth attempt. (Shell/Getty Images)

Monza was designed with that 'goddess of speed' in mind. A sweeping road course of 3.4 miles was connected to a 2.8-mile oval that generated speeds unknown to the hundreds of thousands of Italians who flocked to the spectacle. The first Grand Prix winner was Pietro Bordino, who averaged over 86mph in his scarlet Fiat 804 to lead Nazzaro, his veteran team mate, to an emphatic 1-2 on home soil.

Through its first 77 years, Monza hosted 65 Grands Prix, through which the 'goddess of speed' claimed the lives of nine drivers and 40 spectators. Under the thick green canopy of the surrounding parco, the darkness of those moments remains alongside the triumphs of engineering, skill and bravery that make the Autodromo a focal point of celebration and lamentation in Italy's consciousness, quite unlike any other racing circuit.

Today the banked oval, rebuilt in 1938 and again in 1955, lies crumbling in the woods. Within that ghost circuit is the famous old road course – the sweeping right-handed Curva Grande, the twin right-handed Lesmo corners, the

kink left, Serraglio, the full-blooded left of Vialone that runs out to the back straight, and the long, looping 180° right of Parabolica that brings the cars hurtling back down the wide start/finish straight.

The autodromo may have had chicanes thrust upon it – as they regularly have been since the 1930s – but, where it matters most, the racing line remains unaltered since Bordino's perpendicular Fiat skittered to victory. Unaltered, too, is the devotion and expectation of the Monza faithful: the tifosi.

They come, as they have always come, to cheer their beloved scarlet Italian cars and the men who drive them. After Fiat came Alfa Romeo, and a string of euphoric victories through four decades. By far the longest allegiance, however, has been pledged to the *Cavallino Rampante*, the emblem of a black prancing horse emblazoned on a shield of Modenese yellow, carried on the cars of Scuderia Ferrari.

The tifosi generate a breathless atmosphere beneath the trees of Monza. The tense ambience is unchanged since the drivers stood in readiness on the grid to hear the words 'In

bocca al lupo' – 'go into the wolf's mouth' (and return safely). Monza is where dollars and egos are brushed aside by history, heritage and pride. This place asks each and every driver just how much victory means to them.

Imagine, then, being Michael Schumacher, and arriving at the Autodromo in September 2000.

It was the sixth time he had been there since setting out to achieve something that nobody and nothing – not the coruscating talent of Gilles Villeneuve, nor the iron will of Nigel Mansell, nor even the sublime touch of Alain Prost – had previously managed. He intended to win Ferrari's first Drivers' World Championship since Jody Scheckter and Gilles Villeneuve had howled across the line together at Monza in 1979.

"All I want is a situation where I can develop with a team up to a certain standard," he had said in the heady summer of 1995. "This is a good opportunity to work with Ferrari. In our first season, we will win races. In the second year, we will win the championship."

Back then, the tifosi had gone into open mourning for the end of an era. The longstanding partnership of Jean Alesi and Gerhard Berger that had preceded Schumacher had been nirvana for the Ferrari faithful. Alesi was a pure racer who would carry the nation's hopes on his sleeve. The rakish Berger, a favourite of the late Enzo Ferrari, was both a spiritual anchor and a blisteringly fast driver. Both men had inspired tremendous loyalty from the tifosi by their loyalty to the *Cavallino Rampante*, each epitomising all that a Ferrari Grand Prix driver should be, both in and out of the cockpit.

Schumacher was devastatingly fast, but also controversial. The 1995 season had been a whitewash on the track as Schumacher consummated his second successive World Championship with Benetton, confirming himself as the driver by whose standards all others would be judged – those of Scuderia Ferrari included. When no less a man than Fiat president Gianni Agnelli declared that, if the championship was lost with Schumacher driving, it would be the team's fault, six decades of history were brought to an abrupt halt, and a new order imposed.

At Monza in 1995, while Alesi and Berger had been

Opposite: Monza is the meeting of past and present, and as evocative a stage as any to be found in world sport. (LAT)

Above: At Monza, nothing can stand between the tifosi and their beloved scarlet Ferraris... well, almost nothing. (LAT)

feted by their avidly loyal public, Schumacher had been forced to sneak in and out of the paddock under armed guard. In the race, Alesi had briefly led Berger in a euphoric Ferrari 1-2 around the old Autodromo, but Berger's suspension had been damaged when the TV camera flew off his team mate's car, and then, with five laps to go, flames had burst from the leading Ferrari as a wheel bearing failed. Alesi had crawled back to the pits, where he had gunned its V12 in salute to the packed grandstands. He had sat, sobbing, on the pit wall, opposite a home-made banner that read: 'Jean! Turn your eyes to the sky. It is the only thing bigger than you'.

The following year, Schumacher had made his way through the ornate iron gates in the ancient, golden-yellow walls, and delivered victory in the Gran Premio d'Italia – something that no Ferrari driver had done since Berger had secured an emotionally draining 1-2 with Michele Alboreto in 1988, just weeks after the death of Enzo Ferrari.

Since then, however, Schumacher's two-year plan for domination had been derailed. The victories of his first year

had almost been followed up with the 1997 World Championship but, half an hour from sealing the title at Jerez, the Williams of his title rival, Jacques Villeneuve, had lunged up the inside of the Ferrari. The resulting collision had heaped disgrace on Schumacher, that had only been assuaged by his relentless struggle throughout 1998 against a technically superior McLaren-Mercedes team.

For two years, Schumacher and Ferrari had chased their ambitions to the final round – and lost. In 1999, Ferrari had edged ahead in terms of speed, but Schumacher's season had been written off in a leg-breaking accident at the British Grand Prix. Then came 2000.

Five wins from the first eight races gave Schumacher a 22-point lead before a five-race nightmare of three retirements and two defeats. McLaren's Mika Häkkinen regained the advantage and began a charge towards his third straight Drivers' title, culminating in his victory at Spa-Francorchamps.

In the closing stages of a furious race, Schumacher's leading Ferrari was hunted down by the McLaren and, in a

Arriving at the Autodromo, the team's every step from the sanctuary of the pits or motorhome was met by journalists looking to get that golden quote, and circling photographers. The Ferrari team's tale of reinvention, restructure, controversy and disappointment at the epicentre of Formula One had reached critical mass at the most emotive circuit in the world.

Monza's unique history and atmosphere pervade in subtle ways. Getting to the paddock means passing through tunnels and under bridges, all of which are covered in decades of graffiti. The names of the tifosi's heroes are all here – Mansell, Alesi, Berger and, most of all, Gilles Villeneuve. With every silent 'Forza!' inscribed on the wall there is the question: 'Are you good enough, as good as them?'

From the first free practice session on Friday morning, Ferrari had P1 and P2 on the timing screens, Schumacher ahead of team mate Rubens Barrichello, yet nobody would be drawn into confidently predicting the team's fortunes. Nobody, that is, save Ralf Schumacher, Michael's irreverent little brother, racing for Williams-BMW. "You have to expect it," he said. "Everybody knows they run fast on Friday to sell tickets at the weekend!"

The Ferrari F1-2000s that were brought to Monza had been rebuilt in the 10 days available to the team: revised suspension geometry, a new rear wing, a new floor and a new diffuser were all rushed through after a hectic test programme. Schumacher's car, chassis 205, was the eighth and last of the line. Built in mid-August, it featured all the 'tweaks' to the chassis design that had been discovered through the course of the season.

One extra little addition, barely noticeable among the low-downforce wings and other Monza necessities, was a small sensor attached to the floor of the car, just in front of the rear wheels. Looking a little like a supermarket barcode reader, it was a temperature sensor that would hopefully help the Bridgestone technicians to fix the Achilles' Heel of the F1-2000.

Opposite: The way we were: Jean Alesi in the rich rosso corsa of Scuderia Ferrari, the howl of a V-12 – and promise frequently dashed. (LAT)

Left: At the 2000 Belgian Grand Prix, Schumacher had put up a particularly robust defence against Mika Häkkinen's title charge. After the race, the Finn had a quiet word... (LAT)

moment of desperation, Schumacher attempted to intimidate Häkkinen on the 200mph run up to Les Combes. Next time round, Häkkinen was inspired, using Ricardo Zonta's BAR for cover as he dived inside both cars to win the race.

Schumacher was now six points behind with 40 on the table. It was a big ask, and everything hinged on the Gran Premio d'Italia.

At Maranello, the mood was tense throughout the 10 days between Spa and Monza. "Really there was a shortcoming in the design and the way we set up the car, which meant that our opposition could get an advantage," remembered Ferrari's chief designer, Rory Byrne. "There were some circuits where we were limited by our rear tyres – in other words, the driver couldn't really race as fast as he wanted. He had to race only as fast as the rear tyre consistency would let him. If he pushed too hard, he could go quickly for a lap or two and then the tyres would go off. We weren't as good at that as McLaren – especially in hot conditions. There were quite a few races when they beat us because they were more consistent in the race."

On Friday night, both Schumacher's car and Barrichello's chassis 202 were fitted with the new 049C engine in readiness for qualifying. When the hour came, Schumacher fluffed his first flying lap, forcing him onto the unfashionable schedule of three blocks of four laps, rather than four blocks of three. Yet it was the second flying lap, with the tyres right up at maximum temperature, that proved the fastest each time. Pole belonged to Schumacher by four-tenths of a second – until Barrichello shaded him by 0.014s. The tifosi looked on with relish.

For his final run, Schumacher changed his car to Barrichello's settings and reclaimed the pole. Barrichello finished second, Häkkinen's McLaren third. The Monza faithful went away happy. The German fans got drunk in the forests. The very air grew expectant over the Autodromo.

It was 21 years to the day after Jody Scheckter had last won the title for Ferrari, his coronation coming with that Ferrari 1-2 at Monza. In the autumnal chill, expectant tifosi poured in through, over and around the gates, as ever they had for almost 80 years. Rather than the whisper of 'In bocca al lupo,' the drivers appeared to a fanfare of pop music and parades of beautiful women in spray-on Lycra uniforms.

Some among the drivers looked down to the end of the main straight at the Rettifilio tribune with some trepidation. Shortened and tightened, the first chicane seemed to be just waiting for the first shards of carbonfibre to be spread there in the habitual crush. When the cars finally shot away from the line, however, they did so in generally good order.

Instead, all hell broke loose at the second chicane, Variante della Roggia, through which Schumacher swept ahead of the McLarens of Häkkinen and David Coulthard, with Barrichello's slow-starting Ferrari fending off Jarno Trulli's Jordan. The sister Jordan of Heinz-Harald Frentzen was there too and, in the scrabble under braking from over 200mph, these three cars touched.

Frentzen's Jordan kissed the back of Barrichello's Ferrari, cannoning him into Trulli's Jordan. In an explosion of wheels, bodywork and suspension, the three spinning cars collected the hapless Coulthard as they careened into the gravel trap. Before they had come to rest, a second accident had begun.

Into the chaos and tyre smoke came the midfield and, in the confusion, Pedro de la Rosa's Arrows hit the back of Ricardo Zonta's BAR before launching itself over Johnny Herbert's Jaguar into a series of barrel rolls. Coming back to earth, it clipped Barrichello's helmet before landing upside down with its rear end on top of Coulthard's stricken McLaren.

As de la Rosa burrowed down low in the cockpit, one of his car's wheels came crashing down onto Frentzen's sidepod after flying over 100ft in the air. There was anger and bewilderment aplenty, but none of the seven stranded drivers was hurt. Another narrow escape, it was thought – until the Medical Car glided to a halt where the accidents had begun.

From the circling helicopter, TV pictures were beamed back of a prone figure undergoing heart massage. His name was Paolo Ghislimberti. He was a 33-year-old fire marshal from Trento, recently married, and he was mortally wounded. He had stepped away from the safety of the marshals' post to watch the first rush of cars and, in the one possible instant he could have been there, found himself in the way of a wheel as it flew across the barrier.

The Safety Car was deployed and, in the grandstands, where nobody knew of Ghislimberti's misfortune, Schumacher was cheered each time he droned by at the front of the queue.

There was debris all over the circuit at the Variante della Roggia. Seven cars had been eliminated. There was the certainty of a police investigation as soon as the cars stopped running. The spectre of another Italian tragedy returned to haunt the paddock: before Ghislimberti, the last fatality in Formula One had also come in Italy.

The death of Ayrton Senna at the 1994 San Marino Grand Prix had sparked a three-year investigation and a ten-month hearing: under Italian law, somebody must always be culpable for sporting fatalities.

That day the mantle of the world's greatest racing driver had passed to Schumacher, who arrived at Monza in 2000 with 40 victories to Senna's 41, chasing his third World Championship to equal Senna's tally.

The Safety Car stayed out for 10 laps. The teams busied themselves by calculating their revised fuel loadings and

wrestling the conundrums of reduced tyre wear against the inevitable drops in pressure and temperature.

When the lights finally went off on the Safety Car, Schumacher slowed to a crawl, then accelerated away, then slowed again, bunching and unnerving the field. Jenson Button, the new star of the Williams team, was caught out, forced to swerve away from Jacques Villeneuve's BAR. On grass, the Williams was uncontrollable, clipping the retaining barrier and breaking its suspension.

If Button was short on praise for Schumacher, however, the grandstands erupted as the tifosi readied themselves for a vintage performance by their man, and the team settled down for the definitive race of its season.

On the first racing lap, Schumacher pulled away from Häkkinen's pursuing McLaren to the tune of 1.4 seconds. He stretched that advantage to 3 seconds within four laps. Häkkinen managed to hold the leader, but not to gain. After each had made their pitstops, Schumacher remained 12 seconds clear.

Aware that Häkkinen's McLaren had been adjusted into a more effective trim in the pits, however, Schumacher took no chances. He began to push again and set personal best times lap after lap. It was impressive stuff but, in the background, there was frantic activity as the Ferrari and Bridgestone men tried desperately to work out just how long those problematic rear tyres would last under such a beating.

Everyone was running on Bridgestone's medium compound, rather than the harder, more durable rubber. The tyre technicians calculated that, if the leading Ferrari were to single-stop, it would be touch-and-go as to the survival of its tyres. They urged caution. That was the one thing that Schumacher was incapable of delivering, because Häkkinen was clinging on to the Ferrari, with Ralf Schumacher's Williams in third place over a minute adrift of them.

The German could not relent until the closing stages, allowing Häkkinen to close to within 3.8 seconds as the chequered flag fell.

The Monza faithful went berserk. They flowed onto the track as policemen made their way into the paddock to decide who, if anyone, could be blamed for the death of Paolo Ghislimberti. On his slowing down lap, Schumacher's fists were rarely in the cockpit, so hard was he waving. Once out of the car, he rushed to his team and embraced them all. On the podium – still unaware of the fallen marshal – Schumacher leapt and punched the air, grinning ear-to-ear.

Then came the press conference. Schumacher led Häkkinen and his brother Ralf into the familiar pale blue studio. The interviewer said: "Congratulations, Michael. This is your sixth win of the season, even though the last of them was six races ago. You've done it in front of your home fans and you must be delighted."

"Yes, but 'delighted' is the wrong word," Schumacher grinned. "I have no vocabulary for anything else. I am just happy. I am just exhausted..."

"You may not be aware that this is your 41st victory, which puts you in second place, with Ayrton Senna, in the list of all-time winners. Do these records mean a lot to you?"

A pause. "Yes, it does mean a lot to me..." Suddenly the familiar red cap dropped, and Schumacher's hands flew to his face. The race winner was weeping uncontrollably.

Ralf stared daggers at the interviewer. Häkkinen reached out to console his rival while, in the paddock, Mika's wife Erja watched in disbelief – convinced that Schumacher was trying for an Oscar and, in her opinion, failing.

Oblivious to the drama, the fans surged as a river of scarlet, emblazoned by the *Cavallino Rampante*. Opposite the Ferrari garage, a banner was raised. It read: 'Schumi! Turn your eyes to the sky. it is the only thing bigger than you'.

The Scuderia Ferrari camp closed ranks around team principal Jean Todt, who had built a team that had already proved capable of setting new standards. After season following season of disappointment, the end of Ferrari's road to Damascus was in sight. It would be six months before Michael Schumacher lost another Grand Prix.

A new motor racing era had begun.

Above: Unaware of the fate of marshal Paolo Ghislimberti, a euphoric Schumacher greets his team at the end of a mentally and physically draining victory that ranks as one of his bravest. (LAT)

Left: The first of many: after five years of failure, Michael Schumacher and the Ferrari team entered a period of domination this September day at Monza. (Shell/Getty Images)

AT HOME WITH THE TIFOSI

It is Friday morning, 8 September 2000. Above Monza, the grey sky is filled with smoke from the campfires hidden in the woods, spilling out from the tents and motorhomes parked out on the verdant fringes of the redundant banking of the old Autodromo.

Through the thick, cold air comes the chatter of the day's first VIP-laden helicopters, among it a 'whomp-whomp-whomp' familiar to anyone who has seen a Vietnam war movie. For the Carabinieri, not just any old chopper will do. They want something with a bit of presence to it – so an old Bell Huey remains in service to patrol overhead at the Gran Premio, passing among the shoals of corporate queue-hoppers like a barracuda.

It's all part of the unique Monza experience. Expectation builds steadily from before dawn, until it is shredded by the wail of a lone Formula One engine.

On the inside of the Parabolica there is an old, moss-covered, partially hidden terrace. Generations of tifosi agree that is one of the best places in the world to watch a Grand Prix racing car.

The unseen car wails down the back straight, then – 'blam-blam-blam' – its driver sheds 100mph for the Parabolica. A flash of lurid red, a momentary blast of noise, and it's over. For the Italian fans, it has been worth waiting a whole year for such moments. They smile and laugh with delight.

All around the circuit, the pattern is repeated. Young boys leap, as they have always done, over the fences and through the bushes. The old banked circuit is lined with Ferrari flags, hanging loosely from hundreds of motorhomes from Koblenz, Cologne, Munich and Frankfurt. The Monza faithful have learned to welcome Michael Schumacher's own tifosi – bar the occasional firework and late-night, untuneful bellowing of 'We Are The Champions'. They can be distinguished by their still-new scarlet baseball caps bearing the logo of *Deutsche Vermögensberatung*.

After the first session, the news is good – Ferrari is on the pace right from the start. As the team juggles with its tyre compounds and pressures, wing and damper settings, spring rates, gear ratios and fuel loads, the tifosi of every nationality mill happily around.

Many indulge in a little light shopping, some at the official merchandise units behind the paddock, but most in the shabby collection of market stalls on the road back out of the Villa Reale. Here the prices are better and, as well as Schumacher caps or replica overalls, you might find a real nugget – a missing book from your collection, a photograph of Patrick Tambay's emotional win at Imola in 1983.

There is much to be said for the little enterprises that flourish around the Gran Premio. One enterprising soul has painted a motorcycling helmet in Schumacher's lurid Marlboro colours. Several tifosi line up to have their photographs taken holding it. Lovers of motor racing and its history are to be found in a daze within the little enclave of shops around the Libreria Autodromo, competing to find the most obscure book, marvelling at their youthful memories of cars now exquisitely die-cast.

Just outside the paddock gates, there is a sort of corral, where fans and Formula One people rub shoulders over a 'capucco', away from a furious industry and prying eyes in the paddock. This area would be removed in 2002 when the old, overcrowded pit area was rebuilt. Unlike any other circuit in the world, however, the new architecture would be absorbed into the fabric of Monza, and life would go on as it always had – thank goodness.

Below: 'They also serve, who only stand and wait.' For the Ferrari faithful, Monza each September is a communion with the dreams of the entire Italian nation. (Ferrari)

Chapter Two

IN ENZO'S FOOTSTEPS

"The magic of Ferrari is outside. Inside, there is no magic of Ferrari. We just have to work."

Jean Todt sits at a desk in a bright, open room on the ground floor of the Gestione Sportiva, Ferrari's hallowed racing department. He is surrounded by gigantic photographs of podium celebrations from the last decade, scale models of almost every landmark Ferrari Formula One car, a host of trophies, and the obligatory portrait of Enzo Ferrari on his bookshelf. With an economy of words, he has just summed up the very essence of Scuderia Ferrari that he has spent a decade building and nurturing.

The magic conjured up by the red cars might not have much to do with Todt's day-to-day life, but it exists, sure enough, for anyone who has ever been moved by the sight of a racing car being driven at ten-tenths – as every Ferrari appears in the mind's eye.

To dismiss the magic as myth or media hype might be convenient for Todt. But it remains the enduring legacy of Enzo Ferrari, whose dream of building an all-conquering Grand Prix team Todt has fulfilled possibly beyond the founder's wildest dreams.

In more sanguine moments, Todt grudgingly goes along with the myth. After a decade in charge, and now with a string of World Championship titles, he can probably afford the indulgence occasionally. However the Chaplinesque figure of the most successful leader in the team's 73-year history is unaccustomed to looking backwards.

The epicentre: Jean Todt, at ease within the quiet expanse of his office, reflects on his time as the longest-serving and most successful sporting director of Ferrari's Gestione Sportiva. (LAT)

Todt: "If you love cars, if you love racing cars, the first name that comes into your mind is Ferrari, whether you are Italian, French, English, German, Chinese – whatever. Ferrari is special.

"I thought Ferrari was the best challenge I could have. I did have success in rallying, in long-distance rally-raids, in sportscar racing – but I hadn't been in Formula One. Ferrari was in a very critical position and that made me think more about the challenge, because I knew it would be very difficult. For me, it was the only challenge that would make me keen to stay in motorsport."

The scale of the challenge taken up by Todt in the summer of 1993 was daunting indeed. The central role of the sporting director had first been defined in the 1930s, notably by Alfred Neubauer of Mercedes-Benz, as one of provider to and defender of the engineers who had built the racing cars, and the young men who drove them. Yet in 1993, even the great Neubauer would have been stumped by Ferrari's Gestione Sportiva.

Five years after his death, the aura of the Old Man's reign was still firmly in place. Enzo Ferrari would stay at home and await a post-race telephone call from his *direttore sportivo*, whose job was impossible: to align the limitations of the designers and engineers, the aspirations of the drivers, and above all Ferrari's personal expectations and those of the voracious Italian media, with the realities of the Scuderia's engineering, testing, practice, qualifying and race performances.

Unsurprisingly it often seemed that the most urgent part of the role of the *direttore sportivo* was self-preservation. For years, the media reported epic, if often heroic, under-achievement.

In Ferrari's own experience, there was nothing quite like the hot breath of failure on a man's collar to keep him performing at his best. Consequently success often seemed to happen in spite of the best efforts of the *direttore*

Right: Jean Todt may finally have broken the feudal organisation of Enzo Ferrari's team, but the Old Man's magic lives on whenever the scarlet cars are seen. (LAT)

Opposite: Luca di Montezemolo guided Ferrari to the World Championship when still in his twenties, and was the only man who could begin to plan the route back from obscurity. (LAT)

sportivo, rather than because of him. Then, in 1973, all that changed, at least for a little while.

Eyebrows were raised when the Marquis Luca Cordero di Montezemolo, aged 26, was announced as the new *direttore sportivo*. For all his youth and inexperience, however, Montezemolo enjoyed the patronage of Fiat president Gianni Agnelli and was a trained commercial lawyer who had graduated with honours from Rome University and later the Columbia University in New York. Lean and vital, he looked more like the popular vision of a Grand Prix driver than many on the grid. His own brief competition career had been spent in rallying during his university days, where he had made friends of Lancia's team principal, Cesare Fiorio, and the leading professional co-driver of the day, Jean Todt.

Around this time, Ingegnere Ferrari himself first became aware of the youngster when listening to a radio talkshow called *Chiamate Roma 3131* in the late 1960s. The fledgling lawyer had called in to the show to defend the Scuderia's performances with passion and conviction, using the velvety

the 312B3 was as ill-handling a device as the Scuderia had ever operated. Ferrari even temporarily withdrew from Formula One.

Montezemolo immediately restored Forghieri for 1974 and hired a new lead driver, the hitherto unpromising, 25-year-old Austrian, Niki Lauda. He killed off Ferrari's works sportscar team, which had been pre-eminent through the 1950s and 1960s, to focus the Gestione Sportiva on Formula One alone. It was clear for all to see that a new order had come.

The partnership of Lauda and Montezemolo, together with a revitalised Forghieri, invigorated the Gestione Sportiva and, in turn, Ferrari himself, who visibly revelled in the youthful confidence and candour of his new main men. Forghieri and Lauda went to work that winter on the suspension and weight distribution, and the Austrian finished second in the 312B4's first race, giving Montezemolo's regime instant credibility while Forghieri went to work on the 312T for 1975, with its unique transverse gearbox.

With the 312T, Scuderia Ferrari crushed the opposition. Both the Drivers' and Constructors' titles were restored to Maranello for the first time since John Surtees had taken the spoils in 1964 – although, by the time that Ferrari was savouring this success, its architect was gone. Having rebuilt Scuderia Ferrari, Montezemolo was dispatched on a 17-year tour of duty to the very ends of the Agnelli empire. He was appointed as the Director of External Relations of the Fiat Group, then to lead the first Agnelli challenge for the America's Cup, to take control of the *La Stampa* newspaper, to run the Cinzano distillery, to head the organising committee of the Italia 90 football World Cup, and to manage the RCS Video media group. Then he returned to Maranello in 1992 for probably the biggest job of all – president of Ferrari.

The Formula One team that greeted him in 1992 was far removed from the all-powerful force he had created in the mid-1970s. The overwhelming vacuum left by the death of Enzo Ferrari in the summer of 1988 had proven fertile ground for infighting. The *Cavallino Rampante* had been handed over to the marketing men of Fiat, who had little or

charm for which he has since become renowned. In gratitude, Ferrari sent Montezemolo a copy of his autobiography, *Le mie gioie terribili*, inscribed with his violet ink: 'To Luca di Montezemolo, who has the courage of his words and his actions.'

That courage was sorely needed, given the disarray of the Gestione Sportiva that Montezemolo later inherited. Ferrari, aged 75, was in poor health, and his grip on the Scuderia was slackening. This had allowed lead driver Jacky Ickx to wreak havoc in the team, successfully ousting designer Mauro Forghieri from the ongoing development of his 312 cars, which in six seasons had yet to provide a chassis worthy of the silky and powerful flat-12 boxer engine.

Forghieri's successor, Sandro Colombo, got one thing right when he based his 1973 Ferrari 312B3 on a fully stressed monocoque chassis – fully 10 years after Colin Chapman's Lotus 25 had shown that this was the only way to build a modern Grand Prix car. Nonetheless Colombo never got to grips with weight distribution and, as a result,

no idea what to do with it, and little willingness to take any responsibility.

The result was a chaotic and divisive mess. The technical team was still struggling to get back up to strength after allowing John Barnard to develop and build the 640 of 1989–90 in England. Yet, rather than attempting a sustained rebuilding process, it was committed to running Jean-Claude Migeot's radical, untested, twin-floored F92A for its young drivers, Jean Alesi and Ivan Capelli.

The new president moved swiftly into damage limitation, removing Enzo Ferrari's illegitimate son Piero Lardi Ferrari from the post of *direttore sportivo*, and recalling his old right-hand man, Sante Ghedini, to fill in. Ghedini, in turn, was aided by the familiar, now fire-crinkled face of Niki Lauda as the team adviser and sage – giving everyone in Maranello a lift as the 'dream team' of the mid-1970s was revived.

Outwardly, everyone spoke of there being great potential in the F92A, but inwardly nobody was in any doubt that the car was troublesome, unruly and desperately short of power. The race team was more or less left to sink or swim through the coming season, in which Alesi, driving out of his skin, reached the bottom of the podium only twice, while a frankly bewildered Capelli saw his once-promising Formula One career hurtle into oblivion.

Meanwhile plans were laid for a renaissance. To this end, Montezemolo and Lauda went shopping. Gerhard Berger had been a Ferrari favourite in the late 1980s, winning four Grands Prix before joining McLaren as stalwart support to Ayrton Senna's championship victories in 1990–91. The Austrian brought much-needed experience, the ability to develop a racing car, and proven race-winning potential – in return for an unheard of $10 million a year. It was a seller's market, and Berger made sure he got his worth.

Next was the problem of the technical team. In the end, a simple enough solution was found when Montezemolo dispatched Lauda to bring John Barnard back into the fold. His brief was simple: do whatever you want, but do it right. Barnard's politically charged demand that he must be allowed to remain in England was still in place, but there was hope that, with strong management, it could be contained provided there was an improvement on the disastrous 1992 season.

If anything, it was worse. Given the constraints of time and resource, Barnard's F93A could only be a rework of its predecessor. Although the twin-floor concept was gone, the British team insisted on running the car with advanced electronic systems – 'active' suspension in particular – that had taken the likes of Williams years to perfect, and of which Ferrari had no experience. Lauda and Ghedini were powerless to rein in the pandemonium, and Montezemolo was forced to find a man capable of reuniting Scuderia Ferrari.

He turned to Jean Todt. Born in Paris in February 1946, the son of a doctor, Todt had been captivated by motor cars from a young age by the family Mini-Cooper. The Mini was famous throughout France for its giant-killing exploits on the Monte Carlo Rally through the 1960s, and soon Todt was using the car to begin his competition career, sitting in the passenger seat and navigating while a friend took the wheel.

Soon he was a professional co-driver on the international rally scene, guiding the likes of Jean-François Piot, Rauno Aaltonen and Ove Andersson to victory while taking an active interest in the running of the sport as a drivers' representative at the FIA. In the 1970s, Todt became a leading member of the Talbot team, co-driving Guy Frequelin until the end of 1981 when Talbot won the World Rally Championship for Manufacturers.

"I had decided I would stop, and the opportunity came when the chairman of Peugeot at that time was quite impressed with the results we had with Talbot," Todt recalled. "We discussed whether it would be a good thing for Peugeot to be officially involved in rallying. I managed to convince him and had to build the team from scratch. And the car, which was the 205 Turbo 16, put together quite a bit of success."

There is no trace of irony in Todt's manner when describing what became the seminal Group B rally car of the 1980s. The Peugeot 205 T16 paid no concession to the humble runabout on which it was based. Any resemblance to the regular 205 was superficially moulded into the 'Kevlar' and carbonfibre bodywork, beneath which a tubular steel frame housed four-wheel-drive, racing suspension and a mid-mounted, turbocharged, 1.8-litre engine capable of over 500bhp.

Above: Jean Todt won the World Rally Championship as a works co-driver for Talbot in 1981 (left), and as the mastermind behind Peugeot's back-to-back titles in 1985–86 with the awesome Group B 205T16. (Both LAT)

From 1984 to 1986, Peugeot netted nine World Rally Championship wins, two Drivers' titles and two Manufacturers' championships with the 205 T16, before the Group B formula that it defined was outlawed after it was decreed to be too dangerous. Todt took it to the famous Pikes Peak hillclimb in America and to the gruelling Paris–Dakar rally, both of which it duly won.

For 1990, Peugeot decided to tackle the sportscar scene, aiming for victory at Le Mans against Jaguar, Mercedes-Benz, Toyota *et al.* It was Todt's job to convert his rally-based team personnel to the very different disciplines demanded by track racing.

The all-French V10 Peugeot 905 was fast but frail in its first season in 1991. It won on debut at Fuji, but the TWR Jaguar team moved the goalposts by producing the XJR-14, designed by Ross Brawn. Just as Todt's Peugeot team had done in rallying, so Brawn's Jaguar tore up convention to devastating effect.

"We produced what was really a different type of sportscar to what had been raced until that point," Brawn remembered fondly. "At its first race, it was three seconds a lap faster than anything else. It was just a different approach and I was quite impressed by the way he (Todt) got Peugeot to react to that challenge. By the end of the season, they were giving us a hard time. They saw what was possible and he organised them well enough so that, at least by the end of the year, they were competing for races again."

At the final round in Japan, however, both the Jaguar and the Peugeot were beaten by another V10 car, a Mercedes-Benz driven by young Michael Schumacher.

What Todt did was order a completely new car with much bigger wings and much more grip. As Mercedes focused on a return to Formula One, and TWR bought into the Benetton team – combining the talents of Ross Brawn, Rory Byrne and Michael Schumacher – the 905 *Bis* not only won at Le Mans, but also at Silverstone, Donington, Fuji and Magny-Cours, scooping the World Sportscar Championship. In 1993, Peugeot won Le Mans for a second time.

Behind the scenes, Todt was hungry for a new challenge. He wanted Peugeot to commit his team to the task of winning Grands Prix. He lobbied long and hard to get his way, but was flatly refused.

"For many years, I was not prepared to leave Peugeot until I had felt that I had covered all I could cover in motorsport," Todt said. "I just wanted to do something else in the company. But it was too comfortable for many people just to have me doing what I was doing. Eventually I decided that, as I couldn't do whatever I was thinking, it would be better to do something else – not in motor racing."

Todt was regretful about getting itchy feet. After a decade of success at the head of a team he had personally built and maintained, the ties were physical. "I don't like to change the things around me. I don't like to change myself, my room – if somebody told me I had to go somewhere else, I would be very unhappy. I don't need to have new things – I like to have a have a high standard, but I like simple things, not just what is new. Things must be good, and they must be simple."

This was a far cry from the trauma of Maranello which, in 1993, offered nothing resembling simplicity, and was in dire need of change.

Thankfully for Ferrari, the clear mind and quick eye of the Formula One promotional impresario had spotted Jean Todt. "One day I got a phone call from Bernie Ecclestone telling me that Luca di Montezemolo was asking that I call him," said Todt. "So I called. We had several meetings in Italy and France, and I thought that, if I was to remain in

motor racing, the only place I could really accept to go and enjoy the challenge was Ferrari."

Todt's appointment took many people by surprise, particularly in Italy, where there was pandemonium over the appointment of a non-Italian to command the treasured Gestione Sportiva. As he would ever prove to be, Todt was unmoved by public disquiet and instead began to map out his path towards a new Ferrari era.

When he arrived in Formula One in the summer of 1993, the years of Williams-Renault domination were in full swing, with Alain Prost on his way to repeating Nigel Mansell's dominant title win of the previous year. The memory of McLaren-Honda's domination was still fresh, however. Todt, with Montezemolo's backing, set out on a recruiting drive among McLaren's key staff.

Honda had withdrawn from Formula One at the end of 1992 and its chief competition engine designer, Osamu

Above: Having conquered world rallying and rally-raid marathons like the Paris–Dakar, Todt led Peugeot to victory in the World Sportscar Championship, competing against the Jaguars designed by Ross Brawn and the Mercedes driven by Michael Schumacher. (LAT)

Goto, was at something of a loose end. He had stayed on at the fringes of McLaren's effort for 1993, tweaking the team's customer Ford V8 engine and appraising the Lamborghini V12 as a possible replacement – but now McLaren had done a deal with Peugeot to race its nascent Formula One engine in 1994.

The last thing that Todt wanted was for Peugeot, which had betrayed his ambitions of a complete Peugeot Formula One team, to benefit from Goto's experience. He pounced on the Japanese engineer, who took a spell of 'gardening leave' at a company called Tokyo R&D before joining Ferrari as its head of engine research and development. Then, with Goto tied down and Barnard working on an all-new car for 1994, Todt's next target was clear.

Right: Objects of desire: the World Championship-winning pedigree of engine designer Osamu Goto and racing legend Ayrton Senna made their defection from McLaren a priority to Jean Todt when he arrived at Maranello. (Sutton)

Opposite: John Barnard's McLarens had defined Formula One in the 1980s, although success with Ferrari was harder to come by. (Sutton)

Ferrari had been wooing Ayrton Senna since 1991, when his nemesis, Alain Prost, was its team leader. In 1993, Senna was racing without a contract: McLaren was paying him $1 million per race in a deal from which he could walk away at any time. Todt and Montezemolo did their level best to make him walk in their direction throughout the short space of time available.

It would cost them, of course, but they reckoned that having Senna in a scarlet car would be worth a hundred times what they would be asked to pay out. The triple champion was sorely tempted, but he was hankering after the dominant Williams-Renault and an immediate return to winning championships, rather than spending two or three precious years breathing life into the *Cavallino Rampante*.

Senna could also see that there was a challenger to his throne – not as the World Champion (Nigel Mansell and Alain Prost had consecutively used a Williams-Renault to deny him that honour), but as the acknowledged best driver in Formula One. His personal battle for supremacy with Michael Schumacher was growing more intense and threatening his dream of matching Juan Manuel Fangio's

five titles. Once that was done, however, Senna made it clear that he wanted to drive for Ferrari in 1996.

"I will end my career there," he told his partner, Adriane Galisteu. "Even if Ferrari's car is as slow as a VW Beetle, I still want to be driving it on my last start, my last lap, my last race. Ferrari is the myth of Formula One. The tradition, the soul, the passion…"

For 1994–95, Todt swallowed the disappointment, retained Alesi and Berger, and went to work. Goto joined the engineering stars of Todt's Le Mans winning Peugeot V10 programme, including Christophe Mary and Gilles Simon, and began to build a huge 'brains trust' in the engine department while the British operation continued to lead the chassis development.

The first fruits came in the form of the 1994 412T, which was a considerable step in the right direction. Berger finished third in the championship with Alesi fifth. Todt meanwhile continued to strengthen the technical team, bringing in Minardi technical director Aldo Costa for 1995 to coordinate the chassis design in

Britain and powertrain development in Italy to better effect, while engine expert Paolo Martinelli joined the Gestione Sportiva from the design team of Ferrari's road cars.

"Since the beginning, I had a good relationship and feel with Mr Todt," said Costa. "When I first met him, I thought, 'With this man, I agree 100%.' I always had this impression." Just as well, for it was Costa's role to instill the unity that Todt craved at ground-level, meaning that he had to bridge the gulf that still lingered between Maranello and Barnard's design team in England.

Martinelli, for his part, was quick to see that Todt's way was the right way, as the momentum began to build behind Costa's efforts. "It was in the past a story of Ferrari as a team with a lot of internal conflicts," said Martinelli. "There were many different opinions inside the team – conflict between the engine people here and the chassis people in England. One of the key points of our success has been working as an integrated group under Jean Todt here in Maranello."

As peace threatened to break out on the technical front, so Todt, Lauda and Montezemolo began the job of funding their ambitions by luring the lucrative Marlboro sponsorship away from McLaren. "Philip Morris had to choose between two teams because they could focus only on one," said Todt. "That deal didn't happen just like that, from the sky. When they chose to come with Ferrari, it was the result of a lot of discussions and effort."

Despite all the successes of 21 years with the British team – the titles with Emerson Fittipaldi, James Hunt, Niki Lauda, Alain Prost and Ayrton Senna – the allure of Maranello had long been a preoccupation of the Philip Morris owned cigarette brand. It had contributed to the retainers of Ferrari's drivers since 1973, and now the opportunity to create 'Scuderia Ferrari Marlboro' proved irresistible.

The immediate result of this financial boost was that Ferrari could consider a bid for the services of Michael Schumacher in 1995. Todt sent Niki Lauda as his emissary.

"Niki managed a meeting in Nice with his manager, himself, Niki and myself," said Todt. "We met and then – of course with the agreement of Montezemolo, because it was a strategic choice – I kept everybody at the highest level committed to this resolution."

When Schumacher put pen to paper, it was to the tune of $24 million a year for two years, to be jointly funded by Ferrari, Fiat, Marlboro and petrochemicals giant Shell, whose backing Todt and Montezemolo had also prised away from McLaren.

For Ron Dennis, the ultra-competitive McLaren boss, it seemed Ferrari repeatedly kicked him when he was down in the seasons 1993–94–95. He lost his principal sponsor and his fuel supplier, and finally any hope that his new engine provider, Mercedes-Benz, would bring along the talents of its protégé, Michael Schumacher. All this galvanised his distaste for all things *rosso corsa*.

Todt, meanwhile, could draw breath momentarily, having put the first stage of his plan into place. The second stage was to make up the gulf in performance between Ferrari and the all-conquering Williams-Renault team.

"I think it is normal in life that you get what you put in the ground," he says. "I mean simply it is a result of having most of the people here who are leaders in their field. They have a common vision about things, a common understanding about things. They suffered together, resisted together – it creates a strong link."

The suffering came quickly. For 1996, Ferrari and Schumacher were armed with a new V10 developed by the engine team led by Goto and Simon, but Barnard's F310 chassis proved to be an obstacle. It was essentially a modified 1995 car mated to a new engine and gearbox but, within the first couple of races, the gearbox was shelved, and the chassis in need of substantial reworking.

The Italian press turned on Todt with a vengeance, impatient for Ferrari's revival to take place and embarrassed that Schumacher, with his epic salary and back-to-back titles, was a spectator as Williams-Renault team mates Damon Hill and Jacques Villeneuve battled for the championship.

Schumacher was also dismayed, and he began to lobby hard for a new technical team. Only once (on his stunning debut in the 1991 Belgian Grand Prix for Jordan) had he raced without Ross Brawn watching over him, and the scale of the job at Ferrari was becoming clear. Brawn had also been having a torrid time back at Benetton. His drivers, Ferrari refugees Jean Alesi and Gerhard Berger, were not coping with a car built around Schumacher, who was plainly struggling at Maranello.

"That didn't seem to gel very well initially and I had a phone call, I think about May time, from someone who was close to Michael saying that, if ever I thought about leaving Benetton, would I call them first?" Brawn recalled. "That was really all it was, an offer to have a chat. But a few weeks later I called and asked them what they had in mind…"

At the end of the year, Brawn and Schumacher were reunited, the Englishman basing himself in Italy as the Scuderia's technical director and happy to team up with his old adversary, Jean Todt.

"He was always known as a very straight guy and in the time I've known him he has always been very straight," Brawn said. "He's a good friend to have – and a bad enemy."

Now perceived as the weakest link in the Ferrari chain, Barnard suddenly found himself in the firing line. Brawn and Todt wanted the Gestione Sportiva back under one roof and, as Barnard put the finishing touches to the 1997 car, the F310B – designed at the behest of Todt and Montezemolo to be as close a copy as possible of the Williams – he bade farewell to Ferrari for a second time.

Brawn was meanwhile pushing for another reunion, this time with South African born aerodynamicist Rory Byrne, with whose cars he had guided Schumacher to two World Championships. As had been the case with Brawn, Ferrari found that it was pushing against an open door. "I'd been in England 22 years at that stage and I decided that I'd had great fun, played a lot of cricket, but really I wanted to be immersed in another culture," said Byrne. "At the end of 1996, I looked at business opportunities in scuba diving, and was setting up a school in the Far East."

Any thoughts that Byrne may have entertained of getting away from it all were swiftly dashed, however. "I'd been there about a month and was just starting to get into the issues involved, the practicalities, when the landlady running the chalets where I was staying came over and said: 'There's a phone call for you.' Very few people knew how to get hold of me and I thought there must be some problem with the family back in South Africa. But it was Jean Todt on the other end of the line!"

Finally Todt's mission to rebuild Scuderia Ferrari was taking shape. With the support of Montezemolo and Agnelli above him, he had built the all-new Scuderia Ferrari Marlboro that appeared at the start of 1997. Little or no trace of the old regime remained, and that included Niki Lauda.

Opposite, top left: Joining Ferrari in 1995 was an enormous leap of faith for both Michael Schumacher and Jean Todt that has brought a special bond between the two men. (Shell/Getty Images)

Top right: In order to win the World Championship for Ferrari, Schumacher needed the guiding hand of Ross Brawn alongside him to restore both the Cavallino Rampante *and their glory days together at Benetton.* (Sutton)

Bottom: As the team principal, Jean Todt presides over a large and dedicated workforce at Maranello. (Ferrari)

"He... let's say... he had a position inside Ferrari as a consultant, but he was only really a spectator at the races," Todt said. "For me to have someone [useful] in the company, they must be there. You can't communicate only by phone or fax. You must be on the spot and live with the problems... *live* the problems!"

With the team in place around him, 'living the problems' became Todt's preoccupation throughout the relentless improvement in Ferrari's on-track performance, whether the problems came from within or without, at the racetrack or in the balance book. There are over 900 people in the Gestione Sportiva, from Schumacher to the cleaning lady, and all are Todt's responsibility. The affectionate respect in which he is held is tangible – he is always referred to as *Mister* Todt – to the point where, at times, it seems that it is he, rather than Montezemolo, who has inherited the mantle of Enzo Ferrari.

It is clearly the role he most relishes, at which he excelled

with Peugeot. "With several hundred people, there are a lot of problems for me daily," he says. "If I leave one unsolved and another one unsolved, it will really create a lot of tension, so every time I see that something is wrong, I have to try. Sometimes I discover things I was not at all prepared to know about! Believe me when I say that it's a job which takes all my time."

Behind Todt's bustle, however, lies the relish of doing what he does. While he would scarcely admit as much, one suspects that, when the alarm clock goes off, it is not too hard to alight for another day at the office, as his press officer Luca Colajanni revealed: "I arrived back in Europe at the end of 2002 after Suzuka, and called in to the office. Mister Todt was already here and he said: 'I just got in and looked at the entrance to the factory.'

"You see, we always display a flag for each victory in each season – we put them on poles at the entrance to the factory. And Mister Todt said to me – he was really moved, this is not smoke and mirrors – he said: 'There are 15 flags out there. We've done such a fantastic job. It's history.'"

A VALUABLE INHERITANCE

The memory of Enzo Ferrari's feudal leadership of Scuderia Ferrari – and indeed of the political maëlstrom that immediately followed it – has all but vanished in the decade-long reign of Jean Todt.

Instead of encouraging personal rivalries within the team, anyone found working for their own benefit rather than that of the team would, one suspects, find the remainder of their time at Maranello short and deeply uncomfortable.

Yet the overpowering sense of unity that pervades the Gestione Sportiva comes from the same raw materials with which Ferrari was founded. Perhaps preserved by its

isolation from the incestuous brain trade of the many British-based teams, today the same engineering skill and absolute passion for racing exists among the Scuderia's Italian workforce as it did when the mechanics wore brown overalls and spontaneously broke into song.

Jean Todt has successfully integrated specialists from around the world without watering down that mix, and the reason for that lies in his inheritance from Ferrari.

Nobody is there waiting for a better offer or a bigger paycheque to arrive – as they are elsewhere on a regular basis. Personal pride, nationality and ambition are all secondary to working for that magical name of Ferrari among a team of such calibre, which would doubtless gladden the Old Man's heart almost as much as the unparalleled successes they have achieved.

THE FIRST 'FERRARI ERA'

In its earliest years, Formula One was illuminated by the dying embers of the 1930s. Racing cars were wheeled out of storage at the end of World War 2 and there was an Indian Summer for many of the great names of the sport's 'golden age'.

To move single-seater racing onward, its new governing body, the FIA, created one 'senior' and one 'junior' class. Formula A was a combination of supercharged 1.5-litre or naturally aspirated 4.5-litre machinery that allowed the pre-war cars – British ERAs, French Talbots and Italian Alfa Romeos and Maseratis – back out to race. Formula B was devised for naturally aspirated 2-litre cars with which new manufacturers, teams, designers and drivers could be blooded. Among these was Scuderia Ferrari.

Opposite: Back where it all began: Michael Schumacher tries out Ferrari's first Formula One winner at Silverstone, where the legend of Ferrari's racing prowess took root. (Shell/Getty Images)

For all that it had achieved through the 1930s as Alfa Romeo's Grand Prix team, Ferrari effectively had to start from scratch. Enzo Ferrari hired former Alfa Romeo designer Gioacchino Colombo to create the 1.5-litre V12 supercharged Tipo 125 – the first Grand Prix Ferrari.

They were confronted by the might of Alfa Romeo's factory team, ironically competing with an update of the 158 'Alfetta' that Colombo had conceived and Ferrari had raced in 1937. Displaying power, speed and reliability, the 'Alfetta' was in a class of its own and Ferrari had to find a new solution to reach the top.

In 1949, Formula A was renamed Formula One and Formula B became Formula Two. Through that season, a version of Colombo's engine, developed by talented young designer Aurelio Lampredi, was put to work in Formula Two against a motley collection of British home-built specials and minor European opposition who were often forced to use road car engines.

In 1950, Lampredi's Formula Two car took 14 outright victories from 21 races, establishing Scuderia Ferrari as a credible force in motor racing. He then turned his attention to winning the new Formula One World Championship, by finding answers to the might of the ageless 'Alfettas'.

Lampredi gambled that he could build a 4.5-litre V12 that had enough power to stay close to the shrieking, supercharged Alfas, but consumed far less fuel. When Lampredi's Ferrari 375 appeared, it was the beginning of a hare-and-tortoise battle for supremacy between the two Italian teams.

At the British Grand Prix of 1951, Lampredi's gamble paid off. Froilàn Gonzáles excelled himself at the wheel of a Ferrari 375 to defeat Alfa Romeo, bringing Enzo Ferrari the tears he had longed to shed: "I have killed my mother," he said.

Not everyone was overcome by the sense of occasion. "I don't think there was half the fuss about it at the time as there will be, for instance, when Toyota wins its first Grand Prix," said Sir Stirling Moss. "Back then, we all just got on with the job. It was a significant occasion, but I don't recall any song and dance."

The Ferrari 375 went on to win the next two Grands Prix in the hands of rising star Alberto Ascari. He came close to stealing the World Championship from Juan Manuel Fangio, but the Argentine prevailed and Alfa Romeo, doyen of the sport through four decades, raced unbeaten into retirement.

The announcement that Alfa Romeo was abandoning the sport shook the FIA. With only Ferrari capable of building a competitive Formula One car, there was little alternative for 1952 but to run the World Championship to Formula Two regulations – a move which, if anything, played further into Ferrari's hands.

At the end of the 1951, a shortened 375 Formula One chassis appeared, mated to a gem-like, four-cylinder F2 engine from Lampredi. It was called the Ferrari 500 and it won its first event, the Grand Prix di Modena, by a minute.

The four-cylinder engine offered 180bhp and 155mph – almost 30mph more than the rival Cooper-Bristol. As a result, the World Championships of 1952–53 were a rout, the Ferrari 500 winning 15 of the 16 Formula Two Grands Prix, team leader Ascari taking successive titles.

This was the first dominant era for the Gestione Sportiva but, in 1954, Formula One was reinstated, with a new 2.5-litre formula. Away from the limelight, the old racing department of Mercedes-Benz in Stuttgart was working on its straight-eight W196. A new era was about to overtake Ferrari.

Chapter Three

TAKING CARE OF BUSINESS

Unlike other founders of private racing teams in the 1920s, Enzo Ferrari had little in the way of personal wealth. Instead he sold his idea of a genuine racing business to Alfa Romeo as a means of increasing its presence in the sport. Ferrari offered to operate a secondstring team for wealthy enthusiasts in domestic events, and Alfa Romeo readily agreed to supply its former driver with the cars he needed.

Ferrari then had to find the money to prepare the cars. He tackled Alfredo Caniato, a hemp merchant from Ferrara, and Mario Tadini, a part-time racer from a wealthy family in Bergamo, at a dinner staged by the Auto Club di Bologna in late 1929. By the end of the evening, Ferrari had 130,000 *lire* from the Caniato family and Tadini (who would do the bulk of the driving in the coming season), plus his own career savings of 50,000 *lire*.

Alfa Romeo added 10,000 *lire* to the pot and Ferruccio Testi, the local vet, contributed 5,000 *lire*. Another driver was found in the expedient form of Luigi Scarfiotti, a prominent local politician and Fascist member of the lower chamber of the Italian parliament.

It was enough for Ferrari to start out and, on 1 December 1929, the Società Anonima Scuderia Ferrari opened for business in temporary quarters amid the machine tool workshops of Carlo Gatti on the via Emilia in Modena.

In the hot seat: president Luca di Montezemolo knows that Ferrari lives and dies on its Grand Prix success and that sentiment is of little value in business. (Ferrari)

Through 1930, Ferrari went assiduously about his business, being sure never to bite the hand that fed him by providing too much competition to the works cars of Alfa Corse. It was a hugely profitable season, nonetheless. Ferrari harvested appearance money from 50 entries in 22 events, of which eight produced outright victories, and several more class wins.

At the Banco San Geminiano e San Prospero in Modena, Ferrari won again. Together with his lawyer, Enzo Levi, he delivered an impassioned treatise on why the bank should lend him 1 million *lire*. Overwhelmed, the bank manager loaned him the money, which bought a dray-horse stable at 11 viale Trento e Trieste, and converted it into fully fledged workshops, offices and a small apartment for Ferrari and his wife, Laura.

Around the new workshops, signage was put up for 1931 to reflect the increasing involvement of outside suppliers in Ferrari's project, notably Shell, which put a fuel pump outside the new headquarters. Meanwhile Alfa Corse began to rely more heavily on the Scuderia, regularly loaning its star driver, Tazio Nuvolari, at the cost of 100% of his starting money and 30% of the winnings he accrued.

Despite this arrangement, the successes of Scuderia Ferrari – with and without Nuvolari – yielded another leap in income, with which Ferrari commissioned Ferruccio Testi to put together a book of the photographs he had taken at every race over the previous two years. *Due Anni di Corse* became the start of a long tradition of Ferrari publications circulated among key customers, contacts and investors in Ferrari's ambitions.

Among those who read the book with interest was Count Carlo Felice 'Didi' Trossi, a talented young racer whose family owned a small bank. Trossi bought the original shares of Testi, Tadini and Caniato, and laid the foundations of Ferrari's place at the heart of wealth and aristocracy.

Greater demand for Ferrari's unique business among wealthy young Italian nobles meant expanding it further, to race motorcycles and sports cars as well as Grand Prix machines through 1932. Then, at the end of the year, Alfa Romeo withdrew as a works team, not wishing to be seen to lose its crown in 1933. Now Scuderia Ferrari became a fully fledged Grand Prix team.

To mark its new status, the Scuderia gained a new emblem, the *Cavallino Rampante*, which replaced the four-leafed clover of Alfa Corse on the bonnets of Italy's premier racing cars. Ferrari's engineers – most of them refugees from Alfa – continued developing the existing cars through 1933 with great success, but then in 1934 came the awesome racing cars of Mercedes-Benz and Auto Union, and the Scuderia was overwhelmed.

Ferrari responded with the first car designed and built on his premises – the fearsome, twin-engined Alfa Romeo *Bimotore* – but it was a failure. The Scuderia's greatest success came instead with the outdated P3, when Nuvolari's skill humbled the Reich on home soil at the 1935 German Grand Prix. It was to be the only real highlight, for the little 1.5-litre Tipo 158, developed through 1937 at the workshops in viale Trento e Trieste, was never raced with the *Cavallino Rampante* on its flanks.

By the start of 1938, Benito Mussolini had grown dismayed by the pounding that his scarlet cars – the symbol of Italy's *machismo* and technical mastery – were receiving at the hands of Hitler's Germany. He ordered that changes be made, fast. Scuderia Ferrari was closed down, and the new 158 'Alfettas' were taken over by Alfa Corse, where Ferrari found employment as an embittered and mutinous team director.

After 18 months of failure and considerable infighting, Ferrari left Alfa Romeo forever, setting up a general engineering business at his old workshops. The Auto-Avio Costruzioni business expanded massively in wartime, producing ball-bearings, leading to the purchase of the farm on via Abetone in Maranello, and the construction of a new factory complex that remains at the heart of Ferrari's operations today.

As soon as he could after the war, Ferrari went back to motor racing, and realised his ambitions to become a constructor by creating his road car business and his new Gestione Sportiva. With the same skills with which, 20 years earlier, he had sold his vision of a profitable racing team to investors, Ferrari put his persuasive powers into building up his company's image. He put his V12 Grand Prix engines into production sports cars that were the embodiment of *La Dolce Vita* and Europe's post-war hedonistic affluence.

Although the image of Ferrari rocketed during the 1950s, however, its finances swiftly fell into disrepair under the burden of trying to match Mercedes-Benz and, later, the onslaught of ingenious British designers who were busily developing compact, highly adjustable racing cars on airfield perimeter tracks.

In 1956, Ferrari was forced to accept not only the Lancia D50 race cars, but also considerable funding from Lancia's parent, Fiat Auto, to run them. The sale of production sports cars became still more crucial, although Ferrari cantankerously dismissed his customers as: "Sportsmen, exhibitionists and 50-year-olds." Balancing the successes of the scarlet cars, not only in Formula One but in every major sports car race, against the fiscal demands of running a business, increasingly relied on the Old Man's mystique. He effectively marketed himself as a Machiavellian figure who viewed the world from behind dark glasses. This further entranced the queues of *glitterati* who sought to buy into the myth.

By the mid-1960s, however, commercial realities had again hit home, and Ferrari, in what might generously be called middle age, was tired. Ford Motor Company offered $18 million for 90% of the company, but received an expletive-laden tirade from the Old Man after he had read a clause in the contract stipulating that his racing operation would be scaled down.

The deal was broken, and Ford went to war. The American corporation invested millions of dollars on its own racing programmes in Europe, on a mission to humble the impudent *Cavallino Rampante*. Ford's GT40 overthrew Ferrari at Le Mans. With Cosworth, Ford then set out to become the most successful engine manufacturer in Formula One history with its seminal DFV. And this engine powered British-based constructors like Lotus, Brabham and Tyrrell past Ferrari in the World Championship as the Scuderia reached its nadir.

With his back against the wall, Ferrari turned to Gianni Agnelli and his Fiat empire. They eventually thrashed out a deal in 1969 whereby Agnelli bought 40% of Ferrari – the sports car business – for US$11 million, with 50% remaining in Ferrari's ownership including autonomous control of the Gestione Sportiva. The remaining 10% was to be held by Ferrari's illegitimate son, Piero Lardi, and would become the family's share on Enzo Ferrari's death, when Fiat would assume its full 90% stake and control of the Gestione Sportiva.

When Enzo Ferrari died in August 1988, Fiat duly took control and, after numerous false starts, brought in its champion manager, Luca di Montezemolo, as Ferrari president in 1992.

Aside from the tumbling form of the Formula One team, Montezemolo was also faced with dwindling road car sales in the recession that followed the 1980s economic boom. Undaunted, Montezemolo drew in the funding to support an ambitious programme to put the Gestione Sportiva back on top in Formula One and, trusting Jean Todt to get the racing side of the business right, focused on the automobile business.

During the 1980s, Fiat's Ferrari product range was seen as somewhat lacklustre. The entry-level Mondiale was a dowdy-looking car, the 348 unreliable and unrewarding, and the flagship Testarossa more a boulevard cruiser than an out-and-out sports car. Only the direct intervention of Enzo Ferrari had led to the creation of the era's two traditional Ferrari products – the 288 GTO and its raucous sibling the F40 – but these were rather more works of pride than viable production cars.

Above: Under Luca di Montezemolo, Ferrari and Maserati have never been so healthy. Here Michael

Schumacher poses with all three of his company cars outside Enzo Ferrari's home. (Ferrari)

Opposite: 'Avvocato' Gianni Agnelli, who shattered his leg in an accident in one of Ferrari's road cars

as a youth but never lost his passion for the Cavallino Rampante. (Shell/Getty Images)

Montezemolo could see that the world had moved on since the peak of image-heavy, label-obsessed 1980s opulence, and tailored Ferrari to fit the new climate. A rewarding experience behind the wheel was key, although one to which ordinary road users could aspire, rather than the unashamedly race-derived experience of Ferrari's heyday in the 1950s and 1960s. The result brought about an epochal range of cars that blended style with substance, more driver-friendly products, and even a whiff of practicality.

So it was that the 348 was reincarnated as the F355, and joined by genuine four-seat touring cars such as the 456 GT and 550 Maranello. At the top of the range was the devastating carbonfibre F50, based around key components of the 1990 Formula One car as the emphasis on Formula One lineage grew increasingly prominent. The 355F1 featured a paddle-operated semi-automatic gearbox that has since spread through the range, becoming even more popular than the traditional manual transmission.

"We have always challenged our engineers to do all they can to introduce new features and technologies in our road cars that were derived from racing," Montezemolo declared. "This is a tradition to which we are wholeheartedly committed."

While the product range underwent radical surgery, the Gestione Sportiva was still a world away from the dominance that it has since established, which forced Montezemolo to look elsewhere for prestige. He drafted in Michele Scannavini as his marketing director, and among his many coups was Ferrari's most famous movie appearance in recent years when James Bond returned to the silver screen after a five-year hiatus.

When filming began on *GoldenEye*, no deal was in place with a motor manufacturer to supply the cars, so 007 was restored to his iconic Aston Martin DB5. Something equally exotic had to be found to rub bumpers with him in the car chase around Monte Carlo. And when sexy Russian spy Xenia Onatopp appeared in Bond's mirrors, she did so at the wheel of a scarlet Ferrari F355.

To guard against the increasing numbers of prestige sports cars, Montezemolo bought the Maserati marque in 1993 as a stable-mate to the *Cavallino Rampante*. The exclusivity of Ferrari was retained, meeting its target of 3500 sales per year, while Maserati was successfully rehabilitated, shaking off its long fall from grace and making inroads into the larger Jaguar–Porsche–Mercedes market with its new Ferrari-derived product range, including the 3200GT and Spyder.

With such conspicuous success, a small hint of things to come was the sale, in 1996, of 3% of Fiat's holding in Ferrari-Maserati to a consortium led by an Italian bank, Mediobanca, for $14.7 million. This was seen as a precursor to a full public flotation at a time when the parent company, Fiat Auto, was already showing signs of a serious downturn as even its once impregnable domestic sales were halved.

Ferrari-Maserati's annual turnover had meanwhile rocketed through the late 1990s to around $2 billion. However, Montezemolo fought off an immediate sell-off, determined to see his strategy through, with considerable backing from Gianni Agnelli. If the changes were to be wrung, it was reasoned, there was plenty of

scope for improvement elsewhere rather than simply destroying what worked.

Lancia, which had enjoyed international success with the Delta in the 1980s (and the exotic competition Delta Integrale that won five consecutive World Rally Championships), faded almost out of existence with a decrepit product range. Alfa Romeo's image went skyward when it produced gorgeous small executive cars like the 156, but it failed to break the stranglehold of Audi, BMW and Mercedes-Benz and fell further into unprofitability.

Fiat meanwhile survived on the worldwide sales of its small, stylish city cars and superminis such as the Punto and Seicento. Its larger cars, such as the Marea and Stilo, were largely ignored. With the world teetering on the brink of another recession, the group was already in freefall, but any attempt to close factories or cut back working hours was met with fury from the powerful Italian trade unions.

In 1998, Fiat had hired Paolo Fresco, dubbed 'the Americano' following his time at the head of US defence giant General Electric, as the CEO of its automobile business. Fresco almost immediately sold a 20% stake in Fiat Auto to General Motors for $2.4 billion, with a clause stating that, if the company should fail, GM would assume control of the remaining 80%.

Soon 'The General' was looking at being handed a dead company – in much the same way that it was threatened by a similar agreement with the Korean motor manufacturer, Daewoo – and moved to get the Italians to cut their losses as fast as possible. With a deadline of 2004 and losses ratcheting up to $2 billion by 2002, drastic action was afoot.

Fiat was forced to liquidate its assets, selling off as many peripheral arms as it could. Without Montezemolo's knowledge, those plans included Ferrari-Maserati and, in the summer of 2002, it was announced that a further 34% of the business had been sold to Mediobanca for $768 million.

Opposite, left: Montezemolo has relentlessly pursued the value of Ferrari's unique image to secure its future, including moving into the luxury and fashion industries. Here Schumacher and Todt open the exclusive Ferrari Store in Maranello. (Ferrari)

Opposite, right: The heir of the Agnelli empire, Umberto Agnelli, Gianni's younger brother, controls Fiat Auto, and the crown jewels of Ferrari and the Juventus football club. (Getty Images)

The president was furious not to have been consulted, and let it be publicly known. "Montezemolo is not leaving Ferrari," said the Ferrari president. "It's just a moment for reflection. Enthusiasm and devotion for the company are unchanged. We're ready for new challenges."

At the end of the year, Montezemolo awarded himself a bonus of 18.3 million Euros, and Jean Todt a bonus of 3.2 million Euros. These actions knocked 54% off the annual profits and – by coincidence – damaged the company's value. No one rushed to sell off more of the stock.

Just as in Enzo Ferrari's time, however, the Ferrari name and all its emotive power belie a financially humble operation. Montezemolo's increasing preoccupation has been to find a way to guarantee autonomy. It is something that the company has been chasing for almost 70 years, but it has also never been so tantalisingly close, thanks in no small measure to Jean Todt, Michael Schumacher and Formula One.

Ownership of Ferrari-Maserati has been divided four ways: Fiat retaining 53%, Mediobanca's syndicate holding 27%, Germany's Commerzbank 10% (bought from Mediobanca for $225 million), and the Ferrari family its 10% entrusted to Piero Lardi Ferrari.

Yet still the pressures of Fiat continue to besiege and pressurise Ferrari, and further upheaval was almost guaranteed in January 2003 when Gianni Agnelli, patriarch and protector to all things Fiat, died and left a gaping void at the top of the group.

Umberto Agnelli, Gianni's younger brother, acceded to the head of the family business and instigated a raft of changes, led by the dismissal of Fresco from his post as Fiat CEO. Agnelli also embarked on a round of negotiations with General Motors.

Meanwhile Montezemolo moved to maintain Ferrari-Maserati's future in the heart of prestige products. In 2002, he joined the board of Pinault-Printemps-Redoute, one of France's biggest retail companies and owner of the designer labels Gucci, Yves St Laurent, Boucheron and a variety of other smaller luxury brands. His vision is to make Ferrari a fashion name as well as a

motoring institution, and the Ferrari retail outlets in Maranello and Bologna are the first of a projected worldwide network. A Ferrari theme hotel in Las Vegas is also high on Montezemolo's agenda.

To ensure that his plans can withstand the financial burden, Montezemolo also allied Ferrari with an all-Italian syndicate, Imprenditori Associati, with its base firmly founded in the fashion industry.

The other partners – Fratini, Marzotto, Benetton and Borghetti – account for the production of Calvin Klein, Guess, Hugo Boss, Cotton Belt, Massimo Osti, Marlboro Classics, Gianfranco Ferre, Missoni, Borgofiori, Uomolebole, Principe, Benetton, Playlife and Schops fashions, Limoni, Barbert and BBF cosmetics, and a chunk of the Van Cleef & Arpels diamond business. This high-profile, high-added-value group put together a bid to buy the Italian state tobacco business, EIT, including its own MB brand and the rights to distribute Marlboro. Undoubtedly Imprenditori Associati had the spending power to make an independent motor company.

Meanwhile, from the factory in Maranello, the latest range continues to sell strongly into the 21st century. The F355 has been replaced by the 360 Modena, the F50 by an all-new supercar simply called Enzo.

The latter is a $700,000 flagship, launched in 2002 under a thunderous barrage of linkages and associations with the Formula One team, from its nose – redolent of Rory Byrne's front wings – to the tailored driver's seat for which a pre-delivery fitting is required. The Bridgestone F1 team designed its unique tyres, Brembo developed carbon-ceramic brakes to control it, and the Gestione Sportiva poured in a decade's worth of work into its traction control, 'active' suspension and other gizmos. So the Enzo is perhaps the ultimate performance car. It is certainly imbued with the kind of racing pedigree to which no other manufacturer can aspire.

In today's market, motoring superpowers are lined up against each other. Volkswagen has its stable of brands – Audi, Bentley, Seat, Skoda, VW – in competition with other brand 'families' equally as diverse as its own.

Ferrari. Enzo Ferrari himself would have been thrilled.

Throughout all the turmoil of Fiat and the geopolitics of the world automobile industry, the Gestione Sportiva has remained aloof. It still marches to the beat of its own drum, just as Enzo Ferrari and Gianni Agnelli envisaged back in 1969.

Ferrari has become the definitive motor racing team of the modern era, its success as clear in the balance books as in the history books. It has achieved this through astute management, thanks to the strength of the team formed by Jean Todt, and the independence of Ferrari-Maserati (and especially the Gestione Sportiva) from the parent Fiat Group that was carefully ensured by Montezemolo. While the other manufacturers spend vast sums on trying to get on terms with the scarlet cars, Ferrari has simply continued at its own pace in developing the latest and greatest in Formula One equipment.

The work of the Gestione Sportiva is conducted by a total of approximately 700 people, 150 of whom are engaged in engine development, 50 in aerodynamics, 35 in the chassis, 75 in composites, 200 in other production, 55 in mechanical systems, 40 in electrical systems, 45 in the race team, and 60 in the test team. Unlike many other Formula One teams, Ferrari has not reduced this number in response to the worsening worldwide financial climate, because the funding that maintains these resources is equally formidable.

"For me, it's crucial, but I wouldn't link everything to Philip Morris and Vodafone," said Jean Todt. "Shell came back in 1996 when it was not obvious to return to Ferrari. Then we had some other partners until Vodafone decided to be involved seriously at this level in Formula One – and when they had decided, all the other teams wanted to go with Vodafone. It was big effort to convince them to stay with us, but we managed to give the arguments. Being Ferrari is not enough."

But the power and prestige of the *Cavallino Rampante* can hardly have been mistaken as the backdrop to Todt's sales pitch, particularly in view of the sums required to produce the cars, the teams and the results over which he has presided.

Ford owns Lincoln, Jaguar, Land Rover, Aston Martin and Volvo. GM has Chevrolet, Opel, Vauxhall, Cadillac, Oldsmobile, Fiat, Saab and Daewoo. DaimlerChrysler has Mercedes-Benz, Daimler, Maybach, Chrysler, Dodge, Jeep and Mitsubishi. Renault has Nissan. Peugeot has Citroën. BMW has Mini and Rolls-Royce.

In Formula One, the battle is increasingly centred on these giant automobile manufacturers, rather than independent teams. Renault and Toyota run their own in-house teams, Ford owns Jaguar Racing (and supplies Ford-badged Cosworth 'customer' engines), Mercedes-Benz holds a major stake in McLaren and now owns Ilmor Engineering which develops its engines, BMW supplies engines to WilliamsF1, and Honda is the cornerstone of the BAR team.

Imagine the infuriation of these giant corporations to be beaten hands-down by

For 2002–03, Philip Morris is believed to have been the single biggest contributor to the Scuderia Ferrari Marlboro budget, its Marlboro cigarette brand spending around $65 million per year, of which a third went straight into Michael Schumacher's pay packet. Shell is understood to have added around $26 million a year, again contributing towards the salary of the five-time champion. Fiat invested a sum in the region of $17 million each year, and this figure was all but matched by Vodafone.

Bridgestone also contributes not only to Ferrari's budget, but also to that of the mother company. It has long been suggested that the Japanese tyre manufacturer paid for a multi-million dollar refit of the Scuderia's exclusive test track at Fiorano and that, in return, Bridgestone tyres are original equipment on Fiat Puntos and the Ferrari Enzo supercar alike.

Ferrari's income from its engine supply deal with the Sauber Petronas team for the previous year's engines is in the region of $18 million. To this should be added the Scuderia's share of the Formula One prize fund – and the revenues generated by the sale of TV and radio broadcast rights, image rights, Grand Prix promotion fees, Paddock Club hospitality, trade stand rental fees, catering concessions, championship merchandising and all the other sundries gathered up by Bernie Ecclestone's Formula One group.

The distribution of FOM revenue among the teams was agreed in the original Concorde Agreement of 1982. One of the main adversaries to the agreement at the time was Enzo Ferrari, who thoroughly disapproved of Bernie Ecclestone and the 'English' teams taking any share in the riches that he felt Ferrari did a disproportionate amount to accrue.

Scuderia Ferrari was founded, after all, on its ability to turn appearance and prize money into a profitable business. It is understood that, in order to get Ferrari's somewhat grudging agreement, the distribution among the teams was based on the length of time they have been involved in Formula One and the number of points, victories and championships they have won.

The result is that a landslide share in Formula One's income heads to Maranello, and that a considerable chunk of each year's budget comes from the sport itself. Ecclestone's own publication, *F1 Magazine*, quoted Ferrari's 2001 operating budget as $284.35 million for the year before Vodafone came on board. Although other sponsors (such as Tic Tac and FedEx) have gone, the Vodafone deal more than compensates.

Dollar for dollar, this is, in theory, still a smaller budget than is available to other teams on the grid, most notably West McLaren Mercedes, whose 2001 expenditure Ecclestone's magazine rated at $274.55 million. This is because the all-important engine bill is picked up by Mercedes-Benz. In much the same way, BAR – an under-achiever in its short history – is also well up the field in term of earnings, because it has behind it Honda's $250 million engine programme.

Ferrari, lest we forget, builds the entire racing car within the Gestione Sportiva, and pays its own way in everything.

Certainly, Jean Todt does not feel that Ferrari is over-funded. He always makes it clear that the old legend – to the effect that Ferrari has more money than any of the others dream of – is untrue.

"We are isolated, so everybody thinks that Ferrari has the biggest budget, but we don't have unlimited resources," he said. "No, it's not true. We have a limited budget, which is good. Limited resources, which are sufficient, but we do need to pay attention…

"That's why we need such good partners. Otherwise we would not be able to continue our programmes. This is not the case for other top teams who get free supplies and free support."

Nonetheless, amid the upheavals in the administration of Formula One that have been the backdrop to recent World Championships, the distribution of wealth has been a singular bone of contention for many teams, not least the manufacturer-supported Formula One specialists, such as West McLaren Mercedes and BMW.WilliamsF1.

In recent years, the decibel count of the complaints about how Ecclestone's company shares its income has rocketed, to the point where five of the seven manufacturers – BMW, DaimlerChrysler, Fiat, Ford and Honda – have

Above: Telecommunications giant Vodafone has wide-ranging sporting sponsorship programmes including horse racing and cricket, but the all-conquering Manchester United and Ferrari teams are in the vanguard of its world marketing strategy. (Getty Images/ Laurence Griffiths)

Right: Whenever the wraps come off a new Ferrari Formula One car, the company is quick to remind the public where all that technology is heading for. (Shell/Getty Images)

threatened to establish a 'breakaway' series. Their 'Grand Prix World Championship' would start in 2008, on the expiry of the present Concorde Agreement.

This concept was initially dismissed as a mere bargaining device but, as time has dragged on without any settlement of Formula One's financial future, so the GPWC has gathered momentum.

In 2003, Ferrari was offered a $50 million 'sweetener' to ensure that it jumped ship to the GPWC. This offer served to confirm that even the other manufacturers know that no World Championship is worth winning if it does not include Ferrari.

Whether the claim that Formula One teams see only 23% of the funds raised by commercial exploitation includes Ferrari is a matter of conjecture for all not acquainted with the secrets of the Concorde Agreement. Typically, however, Todt's view is crisp and clear. "I think Ferrari has given a lot to Formula One, like Formula One has given a lot to Ferrari – that's why it's a good combination," he said.

"It has given a lot to all the teams and all the companies involved, and I think that is why I have heard this opinion before I joined Ferrari – and I will hear it again after I leave Ferrari. I think Ferrari deserves a lot of credit and respect for what it has done since the beginning of the championship."

As Todt and the Gestione Sportiva continue to battle for more Grand Prix victories and more titles, Montezemolo will maintain his equally successful campaign to keep the business – Ferrari, Maserati and the Formula One team – on the upward path it has been travelling for over a decade. Never mind the share deals, or the future of Fiat. Never mind the banks, the fashion houses and the tobacco industry. The relationship between the success of Formula One and the success of the Ferrari business remains as crucial now as it was in 1950, when the World Championship was established, four years after Enzo Ferrari had started out as a constructor in his own right.

Below: With as much scarlet in the grandstands as Monza, the American race fans delighted in welcoming Scuderia Ferrari Marlboro to their temple of speed, the Indianapolis Motor Speedway. (LAT)

FERRARI TOWN

There is little possible preparation for visiting Maranello. New York may have Yankee Stadium, home of the world's most famous baseball team. Manchester may have Old Trafford, the home of the world's most famous football team. But for much of the time, these stadia stand empty and hollow, while the communities that they serve bustle about their business.

Motor racing makes its own communities, such as England's much-vaunted 'Motorsport Valley' – home to the McLaren, Williams, Renault, BAR, Jordan and Jaguar Formula One teams. From Surrey to Warwickshire, the arc west of London is filled with quaint villages and local pubs in which everyone knows someone who works in Formula One – but, well, it might be impolite to discuss it.

In the equally rustic plain of the Emilia-Romagna, things are rather different. From Parma to Rovenna, north to the hills around Brescia where the Mille Miglia once ran and south to the Renaissance capital of Florence, motor racing is a meaning of life. And all roads lead to Maranello.

Go to buy some toothpaste in Maranello, and the chemist's window is filled with scarlet, chequered flags and photographs of Michael Schumacher, beaming at you from a podium in a far-off country. Get a parking ticket – which is easy to do – and, from behind the cashier's desk at the police station, Enzo Ferrari peers hawkishly down upon you from behind his dark glasses, in pride of place above the cash box.

Every shop, *bistro, ristorante* and hotel is festooned with Ferrari memorabilia. Of late, Ferrari has added to the festoons with its *faux*-Manhattan coffee shop, 'Maranello Made in Red', the Galleria Ferrari museum, and the Ferrari Store, into which customers walk a Ferrari V10 fanfare, and sign their credit card bills on a plinth inscribed by Michael Schumacher and Rubens Barrichello.

There is no grousing among the Maranello townsfolk about unfair competition: anything that brings in more pilgrims is seen as good for everyone. To be interested in Ferrari is to be interested in Maranello, so visitors are regularly treated to a handshake and a 10% discount: 'You like the coffee? Take a packet home.' It takes civic pride into uncharted territory.

As the Ferrari factory has expanded, so too have the roads around it, their names commemorating the men who put Maranello on the map: the via Alberto Ascari, via Dino Alfieri, via Luigi Musso, via Tazio Nuvolari and, of course, the via Dino Ferrari, down which red-coated technicians make their way all day, every day.

Inmates of the Gestione Sportiva are able to move around *incognito* when away from the track. Nonetheless, they can be spotted tucking into Rossella's legendary pasta in the Montana restaurant, which is like a prop from John Frankenheimer's movie *Grand Prix*.

Few of the team venture into Enzo Ferrari's old haunt, the *Ristorante Cavallino*, just opposite the factory gates. But this is an ideal spot to sit and listen to the sounds that echo from the Fiorano test track just down the road.

Whether cars or people, Maranello provides a life-affirming experience – as many will attest. Andy Gann is one such soul: a master model maker from Bristol, whose work has earned him the challenge of creating quarter-scale replicas of every championship-winning Ferrari and Maserati – plus a few more besides – for the Galleria.

At Maranello, everything stops at Grand Prix time. Victory for the Scuderia means victory for everyone in the town. (Shell/Getty Images)

"It's the most terrifying and exhilarating thing I've ever done," he says happily. "Technically the models have to be perfect, of course, but more than that I've got to capture the spirit of the people, the place. The most important thing is to capture what Ferrari *means*. And that's the most remarkable thing of all."

FERRARI AND AMERICA

Two days after the terrorist attacks on America of 11 September 2001, the Formula One crowd was gathering at Monza. That evening, Scuderia Ferrari Marlboro wheeled out a single F2001 into the pit-lane without a trace of corporate signage on it, or even the *Cavallino Rampante*. The car had a bare black nosecone and empty red bodywork.

"Ferrari has taken the decision to show that it shares a sense of grief with the American people, with whom it has always felt close ties," said a team statement.

At first, its surprised and ever-cynical rivals sniggered that this was a bit over the top, that the Scuderia looked more like a 'junior' team that had run out of budget. Then, one by one, other teams followed suit, and the star-spangled banner appeared in place of sponsor logos. Jaguar painted its engine covers black.

Opposite: Much of Ferrari's success stems from the USA, where an affection for the Cavallino Rampante *dates back to the 1930s.* (Shell/Getty Images)

No other team, though, owes as much to America as Ferrari. The Scuderia's first trip to the USA was in 1936, when a consortium headed by World War 1 flying ace Eddie Rickenbacker revived the Trans-Atlantic battle of the Vanderbilt Cup. A temporary circuit was built on the Roosevelt Flying Field near New York, a dizzying four-mile maze that folded in and around itself where Charles Lindbergh's *Spirit of St Louis* had departed on its epic transatlantic flight of 1927. "We must win in New York," Mussolini told Tazio Nuvolari.

"We will win, *Duce*," the Mantuan replied, and duly took one of the easiest victories of his career against the American dirt track and Indy 500 specials. It was the beginning of an enduring love affair between the Scuderia and America.

At the outbreak of World War 2, racer Luigi Chinetti found himself stranded in the USA. By the end of hostilities, he was married and making a handsome living from selling European cars to wealthy Americans. In search of new models, he called in on Enzo Ferrari's nascent operation, and was heartily impressed. Build five cars and he would sell them, he told Ferrari. Build 20, and he would sell them too.

Chinetti worked hard for Ferrari – not least by giving the Gestione Sportiva its first victory at Le Mans in 1949, single-handedly driving 23 of the 24 hours in a Ferrari 166 sports car. He kept his word on selling the cars as well as racing them, and established America as Ferrari's most important market from the start.

To promote Ferrari's products, Chinetti founded Scuderia NART (North American Racing Team), and won the gruelling Carrera Panamericana epic in 1952 at the wheel of a Ferrari 212 Berlinetta, while also bringing the Formula One team to the Indianapolis 500 – albeit with less success. Chinetti's team became prominent in sports car races at Riverside and Laguna Seca as well as the triple crown of Sebring, Daytona and Le Mans throughout the 1950s. Its apogee came in 1964, when it inadvertently clinched the Formula One World Championship.

Enzo Ferrari had fallen out with both the Italian sporting authorities and the FIA because they had refused to ratify his 250LM sports car for racing. To show his disgust, Ferrari withdrew from Formula One, but John Surtees was poised to clinch the title if he could do well enough in the last two races, in the USA and Mexico. The two little 158s duly appeared, but their scarlet bodywork had been repainted blue-and-white for NART. Surtees and team mate Lorenzo Bandini secured Ferrari's sixth title.

It is Ferrari, then, that has led the way in the return of Formula One to America, at the Indianapolis Motor Speedway. The Midwest had little idea what to make of Formula One in the build-up to the revived United States Grand Prix in September 2000. Its newspapers confidently predicted that Indy's hallowed oval would be filled with people wearing black turtlenecks and smoking Gauloises. But it knew what to make of Ferrari, all right.

Americans love nothing so much as a winner. The fans may have arrived wearing the T-shirts and caps of NASCAR, Indy 500 and CART racers but, by lunchtime, the gigantic grandstands had turned as red as those at Monza and Imola. The magic of 18,000rpm howling from those scarlet cars weaved its spell, and the long romance was rekindled.

Chapter Four

MODERN FOUNDATIONS

Scarlet coachwork and the *Cavallino Rampante* are the symbols of Ferrari but, to get to the substance of any car born in Maranello, from the earliest Tipo 125 of 1947 to the modern 360 Modena and F2003-GA, it is essential to look beneath the flowing lines.

"I have always paid more attention to the engine than the chassis," Ferrari himself said, "struggling to maximise power and engine efficiency in the belief that engine power accounted for more than 50% of success on the track." It was a *modus operandi* to which the Scuderia would cling with great success, often returning to Ferrari's own preference for 12-cylinder engines.

Engine power is dependent on the amount of fuel that can be burned, and harnessing the explosions into useable thrust. Right from the start, Ferrari applied the same engine design strategy that is seen in modern Formula One. When the first Ferrari Formula One car appeared, it had a compact, 1.5-litre V12 engine, the 125 F1, designed by Gioachino Colombo with 'oversquare' cylinders (whose bore was wider than the stroke, allowing the engine to reach higher rpm and thereby to generate more power).

When, almost six decades later, the Ferrari F2003-GA was unveiled, it concealed a brand new engine, the 052. It bucked a trend towards ever more compact engines in Formula One in that, relative to those of its predecessor, its cylinder bores had been fractionally widened. This had the effects of lowering the engine's centre of gravity height, as well as increasing its rpm.

Hundreds of experimental ideas are included in every Formula One engine project, and all must be tested and evaluated before they ever hit the track. (Ferrari)

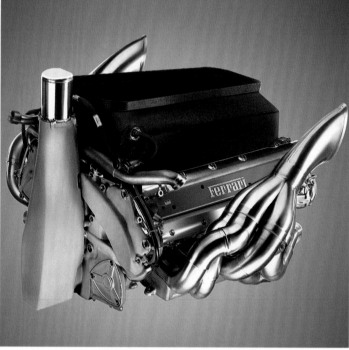

Left: As a constructor, Enzo Ferrari founded his empire on sonorous and powerful engines around which great cars were built. Here he inspects the 312 flat-12 with its creator, Mauro Forghieri. (LAT)

Above: In 2003, the 052 engine was the last word in V10 Formula One engines, using the latest alloy and ceramic materials in its revolutionary design, and capable of achieving 19,000rpm. (Ferrari)

Opposite: Ferrari considered building a V8 Formula One engine during the mid-1990s, its only previous attempt having taken John Surtees to the 1964 World Championship. (LAT)

Ferrari's engine design heritage is not lost on the architect of all Ferrari's V10 engines, Gilles Simon.

"What you cannot avoid, in Ferrari, is that designing the engine is something special," he said. "I have seen recently some engines that are representative of the last 20 years of Ferrari, and you can see how they have made evolutions. You can see features that are in our engines today that were already present 20 years ago. So designing engines for Ferrari is something special."

So too are the engines that Simon himself designs. A modern Formula One V10 is made up of over 5000 individual components, taking over 50 man-hours to assemble, yet it weighs little more than 90kg (200lb). Its crankshaft revolves at approximately 19,000rpm and it generates up to 900bhp. It undertakes 8 million individual combustions in the course of a single race, changing its own oil every 15 seconds, gulping down over 450 litres of air per second, burning a gallon of fuel on every lap.

Ferrari's embrace of the V10 was a long time coming. When the 'turbo era' was discarded in favour of naturally aspirated engines, Ferrari went back to its traditional 12-cylinder layout with the 034. As had ever been the case, more cylinders of shorter stroke meant more rpm and more power to be handled by the radical, semi-automatic gearbox designed by technical director John Barnard.

By the mid-1990s, however, Honda and Renault had shown the virtue of the V10 configuration, winning five straight World Championships before the Ford V8 powered Benetton of Michael Schumacher triumphed in 1994. Ferrari mustered just 10 Grand Prix wins in this period, and finally admitted defeat.

The V12 was heavier and consumed more fuel than the rival V10s and, although it promised more power, it could not deliver enough of an advantage to justify its existence any longer. On his return to the team in 1993, Barnard had seen enough to want to go the light and frugal route, and he recruited fellow Englishman Stuart Groves from Cosworth to produce a Ferrari V8.

The Gestione Sportiva had only ever produced one such engine for Formula One: for the Ferrari 158 that had powered John Surtees to victory in the 1964 World Championship (Fangio's title-winning D50 engine had been a product of Lancia, inherited by Ferrari). However, the 'bigger, better, more, faster' culture that had been fostered from Ferrari's earliest days, allied with the yawning chasm between the 'English' design office and the 'Italian' team, eventually put paid to all Groves's best efforts. Despite a promising study into the possibilities of a Ferrari V8, Groves was soon returned to the fold at Cosworth as Ferrari soldiered on with the latest generation of V12s.

By now Jean Todt was in place at the head of the team, and was determined to follow up any avenue that could restore the *Cavallino Rampante* to its former glory. Having lost Groves, Barnard turned to another British race engine designer, Brian Hart, whose independent V10 was doing great things on a sixpence in the back of Jordan's 194 chassis. With the shift, for 1995, to 3.0-litre engines, the V10 layout was likely to be even more dominant, and Barnard persuaded Claudio Lombardi, the technical director for engines, to take a look.

So urgent was the need for action that there were discussions about simply buying the Hart and badging it as a Ferrari – heresy in Italian eyes. Lombardi won the argument to produce an all-new V12 for the coming season, but ultimately it cost him his job. He was transferred to the road car division. In the opposite direction came a new engine chief, Paolo Martinelli.

"I entered Ferrari in 1978 as a junior engineer working on projects for the injection systems and carburettors for the GT cars, then moved through the areas of engine development and engine design from 1978 to 1994," recalled Martinelli. "Since the introduction of a 3-litre formula in 1995, a continuous evolution of the engine has happened in terms of weight reduction, lowering the centre of gravity and performance improvements."

In 1995, Martinelli presided over a race engine

Right: Paolo Martinelli has spent his entire career designing Ferrari engines for both road and racing cars, and his vast experience has been brought to bear on the Formula One programme since 1995. (Ferrari)

Opposite: Mastering all the technology and resources available to the Gestione Sportiva requires considerable brain power and some of the most advanced computer systems in the world. (Ferrari)

department that was busier than it had been since its earliest days, when Ferrari had worked simultaneously on 1.5-litre and 4.5-litre V12s, and a 2-litre four-cylinder motor. The 041 V12 was developed by former Honda race engine chief Osamu Goto, together with Luca Marmiroli and Christophe Mary from Todt's former Peugeot World Rally Championship team. At the same time, Goto began working on a definitive new V10 with another former Peugeot engineer, Gilles Simon, who had conceived the French company's successful Le Mans V10.

For Todt, it was an enormous logistical burden, and he was glad to have the support of his former Peugeot colleagues alongside the experts from Ferrari. "It's easier at the beginning, particularly when you're running a team of a few hundred people, just to know who will be suited to a position and if they will be happy with that position," he remembered. "So I took a few people from Peugeot. Of course it helped that people like Gilles Simon and Christophe Mary hadn't been as interested in what they had been doing there."

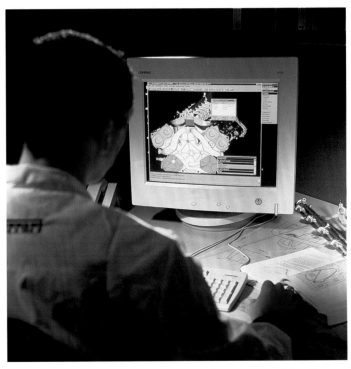

As a starting point, Simon's V10 design proved itself immediately. His 046, developed with Goto and Martinelli, would be 7cm shorter than the old engine and would weigh almost 22kg less.

There was undoubtedly a power deficit, the 1995 V12 having been capable of delivering 760bhp at up to 18,000rpm. Yet, even at the start of its development, the new Ferrari V10 was capable of close to 700bhp, which was deemed adequate. What the 046 lacked in sheer power it made up for in its design, having its cylinder banks set at a 75° angle, and with a lowered centre of gravity height relative to Renault's benchmark RS8, with its 67° spread. Such was its potential that the Renault engineers at Viry-Châtillon were forced to make the first radical changes to their 1997 V10, opening up the RS9 to 76° in recognition of the threat posed by Simon's promising new engine.

Renault, though, was on the way out of Formula One while it was at the top. Although the French manufacturer would doubtless throw everything into one last championship with Williams in 1997, Ferrari's engineers

were working towards the future. So too, however, were the engineers at Ilmor Engineering in Northampton, the manufacturer of Mercedes-Benz badged Formula One engines for McLaren and the instigator of a new technical revolution.

With the parameters of 3-litre V10 technology apparently set, making the most of what was there became the imperative. Ilmor began to experiment with advanced materials in the construction of its engines as early as late 1995. This was also the area into which Paolo Martinelli knew he must steer the Gestione Sportiva to meet the oncoming challenges.

"It's really impressive to me how you can continue to improve year by year," Martinelli said. "The key element is our capacity for improving the design of components as our knowledge grows of the engines themselves. Through the progress of design in a competitive situation, you must optimise the components – the piston, the crankshaft, the conrod and so on. These continuous improvements come in high detail."

The first detail on the agenda of the Formula One front-runners in 1997 was the use of beryllium in making engine components. Prior to Ilmor's engine programme, the main application of this alloy had been in nuclear weapon programmes, where a beryllium cylinder held the plutonium and acted as a neutron reflector that boosted the output of the bomb. For a race engine builder, however, its increased stiffness and dramatic reduction in weight over any other alloy proved to be the decisive factors.

Putting beryllium to work in Formula One meant heavy investment, not least because of the machining process, for which only cubic boron-nitrate tools could be used, and during which the creation of beryllium-oxide dust would prove fatal for anyone who inhaled it. With these hurdles overcome, however, the Mercedes-Benz push to regain its supremacy of the 1930s and 1950s was well under way. Ferrari was forced to fight fire with fire, developing its own aluminium-beryllium engine components through the following seasons.

By now, Martinelli and Simon were also working with a new chassis designer. Unlike Barnard in the previous era,

Rory Byrne was consumed with the need to harness all Ferrari's expertise in one place, and to build future chassis that would be the sum of an overall contribution. The possibilities of the new materials and the new school of engine design offered him enticing prospects for refining the rest of the racecar's layout – its weight distribution, its centre of gravity height and its aerodynamics package.

Gradually the Byrne–Simon alliance began to work towards its goals of producing the lowest possible profile, the optimum balance within the chassis, and the most effective aerodynamics possible. Among the first fruits were Ferrari's revolutionary high-mounted exhausts, flouting the convention of running the hot gases out under the car, which appeared on the F300 in 1998.

As engine speeds escalated, it was necessary to clear the waste gases more efficiently. The complex aerodynamic regime at the back of a Formula One car involves managing gases at more than 800°C within the natural airflow environment. Byrne came up with an ingenious solution, running the exhausts out through the top of the engine cover, throwing the gases out via the shortest route. The shorter exhausts took weight off the rear wheels and altered the weight distribution in favour of the front wheels for which, due to the new adoption of grooved tyres, grip had assumed even greater importance.

Considerable work was needed on the computational fluid dynamics (CFD) computers, in the wind tunnel and on the test tracks to ensure that the hot gases were effectively marshalled. However, as a demonstration of the success of detailed collaboration between the structural, aerodynamics and engine teams at the Gestione Sportiva, the high-mounted exhausts are graphic.

Not that everything has always gone entirely to plan. The 049 engine of 1999 took the radius of the cylinder bores to the extreme, using beryllium to stiffen up the structure, but ultimately the peak RPM were too much for it.

Right: The utmost secrecy surrounds Formula One engines: if you can see one, something has gone wrong somewhere. (Schlegelmilch)

Opposite: Renault has taken the wide-angle route to extremes to optimise its racecar's centre of gravity height, while Ferrari has chosen advanced construction of more conventional engines. (Getty Images/Mark Thompson)

Mercedes-Benz was able to take a step forward in the beryllium race thanks to Ilmor's expertise – by which even Ferrari's technical director, Ross Brawn, was grudgingly impressed. "With a longer stroke, Mercedes reaches the same revs we do," he said. "God knows how they do it."

Nevertheless, Ferrari's 2000 engine achieved a gain of around 15bhp. With this new unit, Brawn, Byrne, Simon and Martinelli completed the formula that would give Michael Schumacher and Ferrari that long-awaited championship.

After life as a chassis designer and aerodynamicist, Brawn found the experience of managing the entire package – engine included – a riveting one. "It has been a very interesting period for me, because I've learned a lot more about engines than I ever knew before coming to Ferrari," he said. "I've had to understand issues involved with engine manufacturing as well as the requirements of car manufacture."

A further component of the successful integration of the Ferrari chassis and its drivetrain has been the gradual

widening of the engine vee-angle from 75° in 1996-97 to 80° in 1998–2000, and on to 90° in 2001–02 before the 92° 052 engine of 2003. This has largely been a response to the arrival of BMW and the return of Renault. The French company decided upon a radical, 111° vee-angle, which has since crept back towards 100° in a quest for reliability.

"Yes, some people are widening their angles but, if you look carefully at their engines – or what you can see from their engines – you can see that it's very possible that we still have a lower centre of gravity," said Gilles Simon. "We opened the angle to a certain extent. To our understanding, it is today more or less the best compromise, but this is linked to our philosophy of how we build the complete car."

Since 2001, Formula One engine designers have been forced to live without the expense of beryllium, because such exotic materials were written out of the FIA Technical Regulations. Even so, they have managed to achieve more RPM, more power and more speed while continuing to shrink the engines and to shed their weight. Metallurgy is as much a part of Formula One development as aerodynamics and tyre development, and Paolo Martinelli's role incorporates making the most of what is available to the engine design team.

"The materials are in continuous evolution," he explained. "You try to optimise the materials for dedicated applications in the engines. Plus the technologies of casting and machining improve year by year.

"We don't directly look at the construction of metals, but we do have good suppliers on the metallurgical side, who are partners to the group. The general technology in the design is another part of the improvement, because the capacity of design is one of continuous evolution. It never stops…"

Metallurgic developments are kept closely under wraps by all the teams, but no one would have been surprised to see Ross Brawn at the 2001 British Grand Prix, deep in conversation with an old friend who happened to work for the US military. Such inroads have been made in the use of titanium, ceramics and other semi-exotic materials that the experience of someone who has designed a nuclear-powered airplane could be very useful indeed – although interpreted within the letter of the Formula One Technical Regulations.

"We have to find new solutions because we want the

engines to progress," noted Simon. "This is our main target, of course, and it is slightly more difficult because you have to take some routes that maybe the metallurgists have not thought of yet! But we do have a requirement for that."

Simon also has requirements for all the engine's ancillary systems to function at the very limits of their capabilities – the electronics and engine management systems, the cooling and hydraulic systems, and the transmission.

Formula One electronics are always a thorny issue. Throughout the first five years of Simon's tenure at Ferrari, there were hints and allegations about the clandestine return of outlawed 'driver-aids' such as traction control and launch control on unnamed cars at the front of the field.

The 'brain' of a Formula One car is its so-called black-box, its electronic control unit. The ECU possesses a massive capacity for acquiring information about the performance of the car's components via a network of sensors. The telemetry system can transmit 4MB of such data in a single burst each time the car passes the team's pit. Such a system is simply too advanced for some observers to take in: fear of the unknown was applied to perspectives of Ferrari's performance advantage to draw dubious conclusions.

A whispering campaign was fuelled in part by the presence of Tad Czapski at the electronics department in Maranello from 1998–2000. The British engineer had earned his reputation as the 'Svengali of the circuit board' at Benetton where, in 1994, Michael Schumacher's championship-winning car was found to be equipped with the now-legendary 'Option 13' program for limiting wheelspin. It was buried, unseen, at the bottom of a 10-option software menu (although it was never proved to have been in use). Allegations of 'elec-trickery' subsequently plagued the nucleus of the Benetton team and, when Czapski moved to Maranello, it did nothing to dispel the fears of the rest of the paddock.

Nevertheless, advanced electronic systems such as 'drive-

by-wire' throttle controls have become increasingly important to Formula One with every passing year, due to the vicious nature of the latest engines. The rush of power generated by a modern racing V10 can be almost beyond the control of human reaction times so, on the grounds of safety, several systems were allowed to remain.

"I really don't know how my engines feel to drive, because I've never driven such an engine," said Simon – without too much regret. "When the driver asks for driveability, to some extent he means what he can 'feel' in the car. The engines in Formula One today behave as though you actually have two engines. One is your lower rpm and the other is your higher rpm. You have a huge change from one to the other, like accelerating with a turbo. When you go through this very steep change in torque, I can imagine that the car would not be driveable. It would not be possible.

"I don't think you can really alter that, because it is due to the way everyone designs these engines today. But you can find a lot of ways of smoothing the transition. It is very difficult to have exactly what the driver requires, from a torque point of view. But it is possible to achieve a slightly better shape of the torque curve."

'Drive-by-wire' was permitted in order to do exactly that, to flatten the torque curve, but under strict FIA policing to ensure that the driver's foot, rather than the computer's brain, was still in command.

Another safety feature endorsed by the FIA has been the pit-lane speed-limiter, which cuts engine rpm to slow the cars as they enter an area where mechanics and officials are exposed. As was the case with 'drive-by-wire', there were fears that it could be adapted to act as a launch control device. So the FIA mandated that the fuel filler caps would open and flashing rear lights would illuminate automatically whenever the program was deployed.

The appearance of sensors around the tyres on some cars, the Ferraris included, also led to speculation. The original traction control systems, like those subsequently developed on road cars, depended on comparing the speed of the driven rear wheels with that of the non-driven front wheels, and reacting to any disparity. Although there to

gauge heat in the tyres – a crucial factor in the case of grooved rubber – it was not too far-fetched for some to believe that the sensors could also be put to different uses.

In 2001 came the 'airbox theory', which suggested that the airspeed and pressure in the engine airbox could be measured against the road speed of the car and the gear ratio that was engaged, so that the onboard computer could select the optimum engine rpm for that speed.

All these theories were entirely feasible. None was totally accurate.

As ever, Ross Brawn relished rolling up his sleeves amid such conundrums and fighting his team's corner. "Part of the theatre of Formula One is that people are turned on by technology, the myth of technology, and that little bit of espionage and gamesmanship that surrounds it all," he said. "I must admit, I am."

The speculation was meat and drink to Brawn, who remained an island of calm amid the furious paddock debate. "If you really start trying to define traction control, it becomes quite difficult," he said. "What is traction

control? At what level of engine management does it become traction control? You could say that traction control is closed-loop control of wheelspin, but it's not that simple. You could have predictive programs and that's what people were into. You could look at the sort of acceleration rate that a tyre could cope with, and map the engine not to exceed that sort of acceleration rate. Was that traction control? Or not?"

Quite. What Ferrari had was an entirely legitimate system that complied with the letter of the law. What was outlawed was any system that took control away from the driver – one that stepped in to counteract wheelspin almost before it happened. Ferrari's software allowed the wheelspin to happen but then responded to it – albeit potentially as little as 0.00001sec later.

The FIA gave Ferrari's 'incipient wheelspin detection' a clean bill of health, but was intensely aware that nobody is in Formula One to be accused of winning by cheating. It decided that, from the 2001 Spanish Grand Prix onwards, it would permit all hitherto outlawed traction control systems, because of the immense problems its technical inspection team had experienced in policing the ban.

The culmination of the relentless development programmes at Maranello came in 2002 when, with technical restrictions of this type a thing of the past, the team reached something close to perfection. Gilles Simon's 051 engine was the product of three years of honing the 90° V10, and it was carried in a product of a parallel programme by Rory Byrne and Aldo Costa in chassis and aerodynamic development.

Also with a revolutionary new gearbox (see sidebar), the Ferrari F2002 was the most mechanically advanced, the most perfectly balanced and aerodynamically the high water mark of Formula One design. Not only that, but it was astonishingly reliable.

The ancient motor racing adage that 'to finish first, first you must finish' was drilled into the Gestione Sportiva at every stage of its rise to pre-eminence. This meant that every new idea had to be exhaustively examined on paper, on the computers, in the wind tunnel, on the dyno and finally on the test track before it ever even got to the race circuit.

As early as 1998, Ferrari Number 2 Eddie Irvine strung together 11 points-scoring finishes, seven of which were on the podium. At its peak of technical dominance, Ferrari logged a record 53 consecutive podium finishes from 53 races to the start of 2003. Michael Schumacher's astonishing 2002 record of never once finishing off the podium in the full 17-race season left Formula One shell-shocked.

From the moment that Jean Todt's technical team was completed in 1997, the momentum of Ferrari has always been carried smoothly upwards. Other teams have taken the initiative on various elements of performance, but all have been frustrated by Ferrari's continuous progress across the board.

"I think the improvements you see and the reliability we make is through a way of work, a method," observed engine technical director Paolo Martinelli. "It's not easy. Sometimes you are pushed to find a solution to finding better performance, but you cannot take this without first proving it is at a proper level of reliability.

"Also, in the current seasons, maybe we have relied on

Above: Early in the 2001 season, accusations of illegal traction control flew, but Ferrari was given a clean bill of health for its interpretation of 'incipient wheelspin limitation'.
(Shell/Getty Images)

Opposite: The heart of Maranello: the engine shop is a bustling place, where Ferrari's tradition of creating amazing race engines is proudly maintained.
(Ferrari)

Rory to design a car that is so fast that we don't need to stress up to the last kilometre of speed in the engine to win a Grand Prix. That is important as well. The continuity of the driver side – having the same people driving our engines for a long period – means we have a long experience of each other, and we know all about the stress these particular drivers put on the engines. That is also part of our reliability story."

In the early races of 2003, just as it had a year earlier, Scuderia Ferrari Marlboro operated an updated version of its former racecar to start the season, while the new car was fettled away from the spotlight. Although the F2003-GA was visibly descended from the F2002, in true Byrne tradition, Simon had again taken a lead in the advances by producing, in the 052, an engine cast entirely in titanium.

The 052 was made possible through the latest advances in rapid prototyping using stereolithography, which allows full-scale, highly detailed components first to be produced in resin, direct from CAD. Complex shapes had been evolved in this way and then cast in titanium for the Trident and Seawolf nuclear submarines, and for the Lockheed Martin/Boeing F-22 fighter aircraft. Italian specialist CRP Technology, in nearby Modena, was among the first to bring this technology to bear in Formula One with the Ferrari and Minardi gearbox housings.

Although costing five times as much as the traditional aluminium casting, the titanium housing was fully viable because it offered the advantage of greater rigidity for lighter weight. This permitted Simon to be adventurous with the 052 by widening the cylinder bore once again – even beyond the point where, in 1999, the engine had failed. The 052 also entered uncharted territory by incorporating the latest thinking in the areas of induction and fuel management.

The cylinder block of the 052 might have been bigger than its predecessor's, but its titanium construction also created an opportunity for further reduction in the size of the rear end of the car, because its extremely rigid construction allowed the suspension to be mounted directly onto the engine.

Although the 052 was 5kg lighter than its predecessor,

Simon actually lengthened it slightly to accommodate its larger-diameter cylinder bores. This meant that the racecar had a longer wheelbase, which again has the general effect of throwing weight forward onto the front wheels. And, in turn, this allowed Byrne to use an extra 500rpm (and 910bhp plus) to best effect, with another reduction in the front wing, and therefore aerodynamic drag.

The F2003-GA also incorporated a range of other detail aerodynamic developments, notably in its curvy sidepods, which had to be repackaged internally to achieve them, and in innovative treatment of its brake ducts and the complex airflow within the wheels.

In just 12 months, the previously ground-breaking F2002 was made to look fussy and overly complex by the the F2003-GA. That said, two heavy accidents that befell Luca Badoer in testing were attributable to the problems of connecting suspension components to surfaces of an engine running at up to 300°C. As Simon admits, such mishaps are part and parcel of the business of dominating Formula One. "I think reliability is not a matter of design, it is a matter of procedures," he says. "You have to test, you have to be sure that you test in representative conditions, and you have to have strong rules on what you race and don't race. This is slightly easier for us, perhaps, because the car as a whole was so strong we didn't have to push the mechanical parts to the last limit to be competitive."

Like the F2002 before it, therefore, the F2003-GA did not make its debut at the first race of the season. As the 2003 season began, it was held back, setting new records of speed and endurance in testing while the F2002 was given its swansong in the first four races. It did not win any of the first three races in Australia, Malaysia and Brazil, but the F2002 was still the class of the field, setting two pole positions and two fastest laps, and only losing what appeared to be certain victories in Australia and Brazil through strategic, rather than mechanical, frailty.

The F2002 and the 051 engine duly won their last race, the 2003 San Marino Grand Prix, before the F2003-GA and the 052 began their competitive careers with back-to-back victories from pole position for Michael Schumacher in the Spanish and Austrian Grands Prix.

Right: Gilles Simon's engines have taken Scuderia Ferrari Marlboro to new levels of pace and durability – and sometimes he is able to enjoy it, as here at the end of the 2002 season in Japan. (Sutton)

Below: Fitting farewell: the amazing Ferrari F2002 and its 051 engine bowed out with victory in the 2003 San Marino Grand Prix. (Ferrari)

BLUE FERRARIS

Perhaps as a legacy of its own humble origins, Scuderia Ferrari has been one of the most active supporters of privateer entrants in the history of Formula One.

As a constructor, Enzo Ferrari's race team was fed and fuelled by sales and, if someone wanted to buy a Grand Prix car rather than a roadgoing sports model, well, the *lire* were just the same. As a result, several of the earliest Grand Prix cars from Maranello raced in French blue, Belgian yellow, the red-and-white of Switzerland, British Racing Green . . .

Recalling Ferrari's early association with Alfa Romeo, a second Ferrari team appeared in 1976 under aspiring young team owner, Giancarlo Minardi. His Scuderia Everest was conceived as a proving ground for young driving talent. It did not take off, but it was Minardi again, 15 years later, who tempted the next customer supply from the Gestione Sportiva to finish seventh out of 18 teams in the 1991 Constructors' championship – the little Faenza team's best-ever result.

In recent years, Ferrari has become associated with the Swiss team, Sauber Petronas. Having lost his works Ford engine deal to the nascent Stewart Grand Prix team in 1996, Peter Sauber initially intended to design and build a new engine in-house for his major sponsor, the Malaysian state petrochemical giant, Petronas. In the interim, however, he needed to find a proven engine and had plenty of funding to cover the cost. So he called Jean Todt.

It took a good deal of negotiation to prise the engines from Ferrari, which was still rebuilding towards a championship challenge. "It really is to Sauber's credit because, when they first came to see me, I told them there was no way we could supply them with an engine," Todt recalled.

"But they put so much pressure on me, and I must say that Peter Sauber is a great guy – one of the fairest, most honest, most loyal people in our sport. So: although they were having problems to find an engine, they had the financial resources to

pay for it and, at the end of the day, after talking with our people, we decided that we could do it without compromising our organisation. And have some benefits…"

Those benefits have become more obvious the longer this relationship has continued. Initially, along with the engine deal for 1997, Sauber took on Osamu Goto, nominally to run the Ferrari engines, but also to put his experience from Honda and Ferrari to work in producing a bespoke Petronas V10. However, such grand plans were shelved indefinitely as a consequence of the economic collapse in the Far East. Instead, a long and profitable relationship for Ferrari was further extended.

For 2001, Goto was given permission for the first time to upgrade the engines beyond the specification in which they arrived at the Sauber HQ in Hinwil, near Zurich. That season, the 'customer' V10 was the upgraded 049 used by Michael Schumacher to win the 2000 Italian Grand Prix. An exceptional Sauber C20 chassis, and an inspired driver pairing of Kimi Räikkönen and Nick Heidfeld, produced the team's best-ever season, taking 21 points and fourth place in the Constructors' championship.

The 2001 season also brought the nadir of Ferrari's 'customer' operation with four-time champion Alain Prost's eponymous team. Having lost almost all his sponsorship, Prost sold 40% of the team to the Diniz family (Brazilian supermarket magnates) in order to raise the funds to lease Ferrari's 2000 engine, gearbox and rear suspension. The cost – around US$18 million – was justified merely by the hope that strong race results would inevitably follow, and that more funds would be forthcoming, thus ensuring the team's future… But it was not to be.

Despite its Ferrari pedigree, the Prost AP04 failed miserably. Meanwhile the world economy slowed to a flickering pulse and, even among the top teams, budgets were shrinking. The Frenchman was powerless to stop his team going to the wall, and Ferrari could not help.

"The Prost position was of course a sadness, and it was damaging, but more to him than to us," said Todt. "We could not afford to lose money on one engine, one gearbox, on providing services to anybody. Everybody thinks that Ferrari has the biggest budget, but we don't have unlimited resources. That's not true."

Opposite, top: Happy customers: Sauber and Ferrari have forged a mutually beneficial relationship through the supply of Petronas-badged engines from Maranello. (Shell/Getty Images)

Opposite, bottom: Alain Prost gambled the future of his team on buying a supply of Ferrari engines in 2001. Here Luciano Burti is launched over Michael Schumacher's nearly stationary Ferrari (right) at Hockenheim. (LAT)

A SHIFTY BUSINESS

When the FIA lifted the 'driver-aid' technology ban in 2001, it offered another avenue for the Gestione Sportiva to explore: the transmission.

Before the ban had come into force at the end of 1993, the transmission had been particularly fertile ground for Formula One innovators. Williams, for example, had even tried a continuously variable transmission. CVT uses a belt that slides up and down a cone-shaped pulley, thereby allowing a single, infinitely adjustable gear ratio. It was hardly a new idea, even in motor racing – Dutch car maker DAF had used it to win Formula Three races way back in 1967. But, in Formula One, it was potentially devastating to keep the engine at its peak torque and power output irrespective of the road speeds or the forces of acceleration or deceleration being applied. Ultimately, however, CVT was one of many transmission concepts that did not work.

Sweet and low: the Brabham BT55 scored only two points in 1986, but it laid the foundations of the two most successful Formula One cars in history: the McLaren MP4-4 and the Ferrari F2002. (Sutton)

The seven-speed transmission produced for the Ferrari F2002 was housed in a smaller casing than any previous Formula One gearbox. When the new car appeared, eyebrows were raised. It was unbelievably low-slung, offering the smallest possible resistance to the air and making even its illustrious predecessors look antiquated. For Ferrari's rivals, the quest to acquire its secrets became all-consuming.

It was obvious that Rory Byrne's design hinged on the revolutionary, new tiny, cast titanium gearbox housing – new to Ferrari, that is, because a prototype had been successfully run in the Minardi M02 in 2000-01. The gearbox was the key to Byrne achieving his long-held ambition of placing the car's centre of gravity height just 23cm above the track surface.

No Formula One car had ever been so low to the ground, with one possible exception: Gordon Murray's Brabham BT55 of 1986. Murray's design had also been built around a tiny gearbox that housed seven gear ratios – the first in Formula One. The BT55 transmission was the work of the late American drivetrain designer Pete Weismann, whose wife had once worked at Ferrari under Carlo Chiti.

Devised for Indianapolis racers in the 1960s, the famous 'Weismann Locker', equipped with an automatic transaxle to allow what amount to 'clutchless' gearshifts without ever engaging neutral, had made its Formula One debut as far back as 1966, when Jack Brabham became the first (and so far only) man to win the World Championship in a car of his own creation.

Two decades later, and Murray's Brabham was powered by BMW's awesome, turbocharged, 1.5-litre straight-four, which was based on one of the Bavarian manufacturer's production engines, and was somewhat bulky as a result. In order to reduce the frontal area of the BT55 and offer a clean airflow to the rear wing, Murray tipped this engine over by 72° in the monocoque. Then he

fitted it with an updated version of the 1966 gearbox. On paper, it was inspired, but unreliability plagued this particular revolution: Bernie Ecclestone's team scored just one point all season.

Undeterred, Murray continued to pursue his low-line concept when he joined McLaren and produced the MP4-4 of 1988, which won 15 out of 16 races and, like the BT55, had a version of the 'Weismann Locker' transmission. In 2002 the Weismann idea seemed to have been revived. "When that new Ferrari came out, and I heard the speed of the gearshifts, I was very concerned that, somehow, someone had come up with a gearbox that was on a par with our 'Quickshift'," recalled Chris Weismann, who now runs his father's business.

"After a few races, it was confirmed that they were in fact running a system just like ours, with a roller clutch rather than the traditional 'dogs' so it that it was able to change gear instantaneously. It seems that a former Williams gearbox engineer had designed it for them."

Unlike Murray's cars, however, the F2002 had the luxury of being designed without compromise. Just as Brawn, Byrne, Simon and Martinelli had planned it, the reduction in bulk at the rear not only aided the car's aerodynamic performance but also its stability, through the optimum weight distribution. The F2002 did not need massive aerodynamic grip to achieve its astonishing on-track composure. Less wing meant less drag, and this in turn meant more straightline speed – an effective counter to the brute power of the latest BMW and Mercedes-Benz engines.

"The transmission was probably the biggest single thing in that it was a lot smaller," said Byrne. "It was shorter, it was narrower, it was a lot lighter, and it had a much smoother, faster gearshift. We could look again at all the fundamentals: the gear selection mechanism was different, as well as the casing material and the casing manufacturing method. The whole thing was integrated into a package in which each element was totally new – not just in detail, but fundamentally."

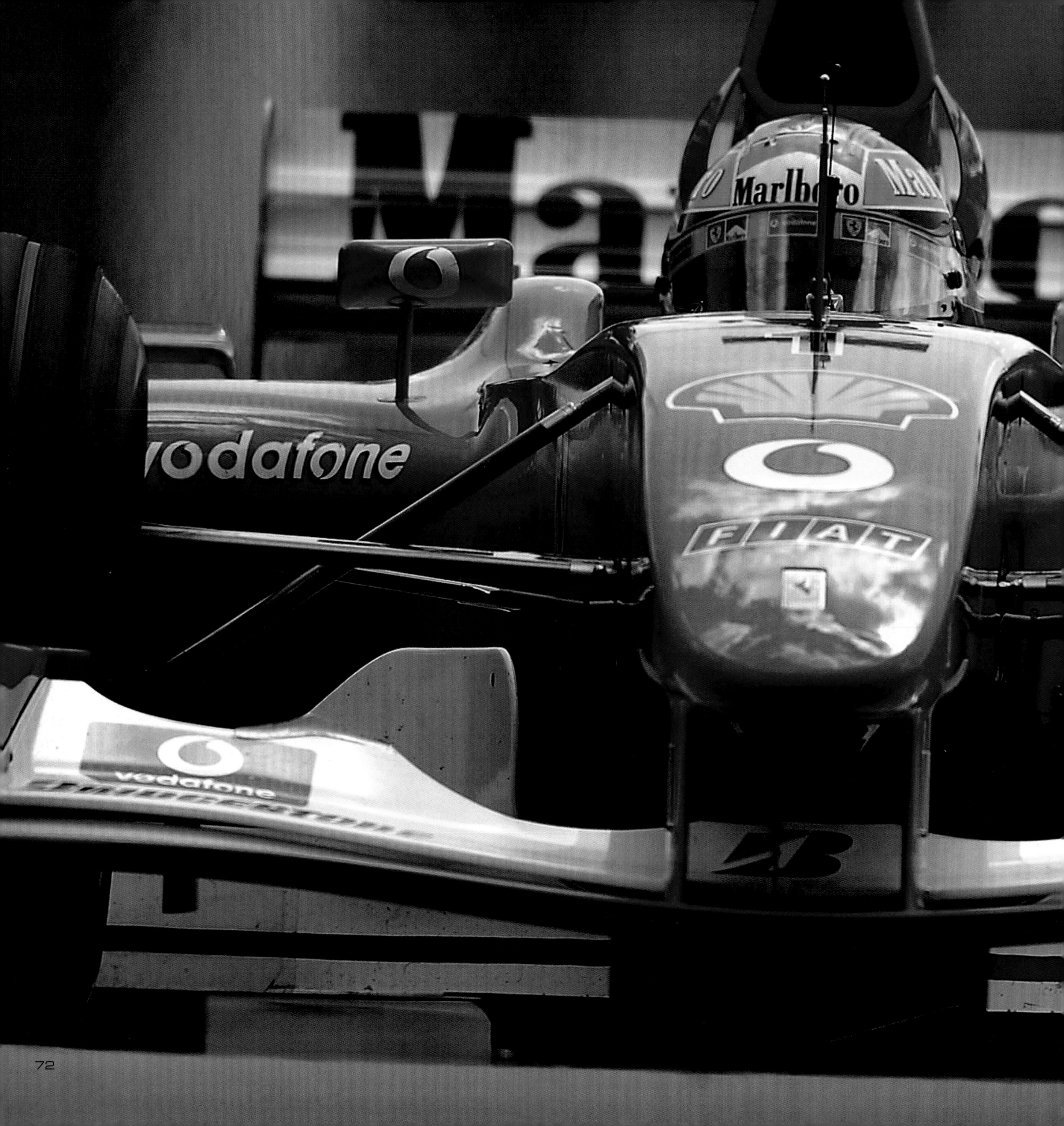
Marlboro
vodafone
FIAT
vodafone

Chapter Five

DRESSED IN RED

A few days before Christmas 2002 Maranello is a grey, damp place, its inhabitants smothered in scarves and tweed in their efforts to hold a sapping chill at bay. But in the Gestione Sportiva, despite a little frailty after the Christmas party and celebrations of their record-breaking season, the staff have a warm and satisfied glow.

All that they had learnt in the course of that season, on top of so many other seasons, had been built into the 2003 Ferrari. All the signs pointed to something special – how special, nobody quite knew – but like an expectant mother looking at the grey smudge of an ultrasound image, they knew that the vital signs were good. "If the numbers we are getting on the computer are right, we'll see our biggest step forward yet," said technical director Ross Brawn. "We're looking at up to a second and a half over the 2002 car."

The new car existed as just so many bytes on a hard drive, with a few top-secret components ready-made on the shop floor, or hidden away in the test mules. Two months later, the Ferrari F2003-GA – named after the later patriarch Gianni Agnelli, who died in January – appeared to a deluge of superlatives. Making its debut at the Spanish Grand Prix in May, the F2003-GA took pole position, fastest lap and put both Michael Schumacher and Rubens Barrichello on the podium, picking up the baton from the all-conquering F2002.

The foundations of the Ferrari F2003-GA were laid in the torrid summer of 1997. Ross Brawn and Rory Byrne were in

Red star rising: the Ferrari F2002 is one of the greatest Formula One cars ever to have turned a wheel. (Shell/Getty Images)

place, charged with turning the years of expertise gained from small, efficient British teams, into rebuilding the Gestione Sportiva as the finest specialist engineering firm in the world.

"It was a culture shock after the small British teams we were used to," remembered Rory Byrne. "I was amazed at the capacity – that was the thing that did strike me. In the true sense of the word, the capacity here is incredible. Obviously, it wasn't all being used to its fullest extent, and that's one thing that has happened over the last few years."

Right: A rare appearance at the races for Rory Byrne, who prefers to stay in Maranello feeding the results of each weekend into the concepts of his next design. (Ferrari)

In 1996, Schumacher arrived and delivered three race wins – more than Ferrari had mustered in the previous four seasons. Those victories were due to Schumacher's individual brilliance, over and above Ferrari's capacity to mount a sustained challenge for World Championships, and the pressure to succeed was mounting daily. Schumacher, as the world's best racing driver, expected the best. Fiat and the other investors expected a return on the massive outlay – as too did the *tifosi* and the rabid Italian media.

Opposite: The start of the modern era came at the 1996 Australian Grand Prix, when Michael Schumacher, Eddie Irvine and the V10 engine made their debuts for the Scuderia. (Shell/Getty Images)

The weakest link was judged to be Ferrari's F310 chassis, designed by John Barnard under the conditions of his geographically distant relationship with the rest of the Gestione Sportiva. Schumacher's driving style – on which the future of Ferrari and billions of dollars had been staked – was simply at odds with the thinking of a designer whose halcyon days had come in the 'turbo' era, when all the attention had been focused on transmitting 1500 horsepower onto the asphalt.

In the 'turbo' days, when Barnard's McLaren-TAG MP4-4 had conquered the world, drivers would turn into a corner relatively slowly, and exit in an explosion of power, steering on the throttle. The greatest exponent of Barnard's McLarens had been Alain Prost, who could make the control of such incendiary violence appear effortlessly graceful. By 1996, all that was a distant memory.

Schumacher's thoroughly modern driving style was founded in cars with half the power and a preponderance of high-tech solutions to the business of going quickly. He demanded that the car was razor-sharp at the front-end, capable of carrying hitherto unheard-of speed into every corner without going off-line. He would ensure that the rest of the car followed apace, either by dint of his own natural gifts or by judicious use of traction control.

After just three months of driving Barnard's car, Schumacher could see that it was not a happy marriage, and began lobbying hard for his former Benetton team mates to join him in Maranello. "I think perhaps the reason I got the phone call was that the team wasn't quite gelling, and of course Michael had joined and he was able to judge how it functioned in comparison with another team," reflected Ross Brawn, who joined as the technical director at the end of 1996.

"I guess Michael was the catalyst to look at things again – to see if there was a better way of doing things. When I

joined Ferrari, the view was: 'We think we want to bring the design in-house – what do you think?' For me, there was no contest. The strength of Ferrari has to be that we can build our own car and our own engine.

"By combining the two, you can produce the ultimate package. I know that people talk a lot about 'packages' but to be able to design the engine and the chassis, and put them together as a racing car, is the best solution."

Rory Byrne followed Brawn early in the New Year. They inherited the 1997 car, the F310B, from the outgoing Barnard and, as a result, the season, technically speaking, was a transitional affair. "We had to cope with the 1997 season and, at the same time, build up a team of people who could design the 1998 car," Brawn recalled of one of the busiest spells of his career.

Right: Ideal anchorman: Aldo Costa's ability to create structures – in terms of both chassis design and project management – have been invaluable to Ferrari's success story. (Ferrari)

Opposite: John Barnard created the F310B for 1997, and then Ross Brawn and Rory Byrne made it a genuine Williams-beater. (Shell/Getty Images)

"Luckily, Aldo Costa was already here, supporting the design work on the Italian side. While most of the work was done in England, Aldo was a key player, and has continued to be a very important person in our organisation. He helped us to bring together a group of designers, technicians and staff to recentralise Ferrari as an organisation."

One of the unsung heroes of the Gestione Sportiva, Costa's relationship with Ferrari goes back to the mid-1980s.

"I did a thesis in Ferrari, my tutor was Giorgio Ascanelli," he said. "My thesis was about suspension and we tried to run new software which, at the time, was a real novelty. That was a good thing to manage. There wasn't really any CAD system for suspension being used at that time. It was one of the first applications for suspension design."

A glittering career with Ferrari eluded Costa at first, however. His arrival coincided with the appointment of John Barnard as the technical director and the migration of Ferrari's design office to Surrey. Keen to keep his burgeoning talent to hand, the Fiat hierarchy found room for Costa at Abarth, and his mentor Ascanelli followed him

there. "We were designing the Lancia Delta Integrale, which was a pretty successful rally car!" he laughed.

Five World Rally Championship titles later, and Lancia withdrew from competition. Costa made his way back to his first love of Formula One, albeit still a few miles away from Maranello – at Faënza with the Minardi team. "For me it was fun and, from a radical point of view, there was much more development going on with the chassis than with the engine – which was a bit of a change from the 1980s.

"I had a lot of things to do because, when I arrived at Minardi, they were not using a wind tunnel, nor even a CAD system. They were not using any modern machining facilities. Telemetry and data-acquisition were not in place on the car because everything was at the start for Minardi. But, when I left, all these modern systems were in place and working quite well. So I had the possibility to force through the development of a modern Formula One team from a white sheet of paper."

By 1995, Todt's grand plan to dominate Formula One

was beginning to take shape, and Ascanelli was in place running the race team. Among the first preparations to take back the design of the cars from Barnard's office in 1996 was Ascanelli's recommendation to Todt that Costa should be brought in from his post as the technical director at Minardi, to build up a new chassis team in the new Gestione Sportiva.

"It was difficult finding new people," Costa continued. "Except for a few aerodynamicists from the Barnard group who came back to Maranello, there were no other engineers who came back. The challenge was to find enough people to work in the design office. In the design office, you need different people at different levels – if you have 100% very talented and strong engineers, then they all want to manage the group, and nobody wants to design anything!

"So you need to have a good blend of experience and youth, and a good mix of ideas. We were very successful in finding people from different environments, not only Formula One or motor racing but from aeronautics, road cars, motorbikes, so that we could have a very nice group in the design office. I didn't look only in one university, but in many, and at different nationalities. We didn't want to concentrate only in Italy, and not only in motor racing. We wanted the best designers and we wanted a good blend."

Having Costa in place allowed Ferrari to do battle for the 1997 championship. Not only was he in charge of scouting out the world's finest young talent to staff the Gestione Sportiva, but he was also able to get on with the layout of the 1998 car, allowing Rory Byrne to hone the F310B that Barnard had delivered for the coming season.

The V10 achieved more power and a lower centre of gravity height but, once again, the chassis lacked early promise. Against it stood the Williams-Renault FW19, the last in the long line of the team's Adrian Newey designed 'supercars'. By the time that the FW19 was delivered, Newey himself was officially on 'gardening leave', having been head-hunted by McLaren International. Even so, at the first race in Melbourne, Williams team leader Jacques Villeneuve took the pole, his lap-time over two seconds clear of Schumacher's Ferrari.

Schumacher was still wrestling with a paucity of front-end grip, forcing the team to crank on as much wing as it dared, and to run incredibly stiff suspension in its efforts to bolt the nose onto the road. This set-up made for a wild, tyre-shredding ride. In a straight line, the Ferrari was a mobile chicane. Yet Brawn's team was undaunted, throwing itself into contention by every means at its disposal.

In 1997, Ferrari was on its way up – preparing for greatness. Williams was on its way down – increasingly forced to accept that a drop in its form was inevitable in seasons to come without Renault power and Newey's chassis design genius. In 1997, the graphs crossed. These teams engaged in often fraught and sometimes bitter combat. By halfway through the season, Schumacher had both the championship lead and a new, lightweight F310B chassis.

Schumacher was less than fully confident in the lightweight car but, despite a resurgent Villeneuve, he kept ahead in the points table. At the penultimate round came a belated cure for the Ferrari's wayward front-end: Byrne

produced a flexible front wing that was located at the legal height in scrutineering, but dropped down closer to the asphalt under airflow pressure. The device glued the car to the road in the high-speed corners that had been the car's Achilles' Heel.

The denouement came at the final round in Jerez, when Schumacher's infamous, petulant lunge at Villeneuve destroyed a season's hard work. He and Ferrari were roundly castigated by the press, the public and the FIA, which stripped the German of all his points from the year (but let him 'keep' his five wins).

At Maranello, however, the technical team was too busy to notice. It remained unruffled as it put the finishing touches to its 1998 car.

"If we had won then, we wouldn't have had the longevity that we have seen now," Brawn observed. "People here remember how tough those years were – 1997–98–99. We were in contention until the last races of those championships and, in a funny way, I think it has made the organisation stronger today. We don't forget those days so we don't forget how hard it is to succeed in Formula One. We know how hard we've worked for what we've achieved, and we don't want to let go of it."

The first genuine Rory Byrne chassis to be put at the disposal of Schumacher and Brawn was the F300 of 1998. So eager was he to put the previous season behind him that Schumacher was in the car early, getting out for a shakedown at Fiorano a few days before Christmas.

Relative to the F310B, the F300 was born of an entirely different era, in the sense that there had been an upheaval in the FIA Technical Regulations in an effort to reduce spiralling cornering speeds. The governing body ruled that the maximum permissible width of the cars was to be drastically reduced – from 200cm to 180cm – while the treadless 'slick' tyres were banished. Instead, grooves in the tyre surfaces reduced the contact patch and therefore grip. Further safety-orientated regulations were aimed at making wider, stronger survival cells with greater rollover protection, with mandatory side-impact testing, while all suspension parts were to be removed from the footwell.

Finally came 'policing' regulations intended to achieve as level a playing field as possible. A prohibition on the use of exotic materials killed off Ferrari's new eight-piston beryllium brake calipers. All electronic methods of altering the front:rear brake balance were also banned, to remove all temptation to deploy the technology to achieve a form of traction control.

As a result everyone, Ferrari included, went into the new season blind. "For 1998, there was a big change of rules – quite considerable changes that really meant a fresh approach in a number of areas," Byrne recalled. "Naturally the 1998 car was quite different from the 1997 car but, although the new rules offered something of a clean-sheet, in essence we still kept the good points from the car we had developed through 1997, and possibly improved on them. Certainly we corrected the bad points and really adapted the package to suit the new regulations. So it was still an evolution, even though the car looked considerably different."

The 'look' of the F300 that Byrne created was to become extremely familiar, with its nose cranked up high, and splitters and scallops carving up the air as effectively as possible. Yet it was the revised suspension and tyre rules that made the F300 what it was. Byrne and his design team strove to find the optimum weight distribution and suspension layout in their scrabble to reclaim lost grip.

The aerodynamic package accomplished a lot, generating over 1500kg of downforce at 150mph. Even so, the tyre performance and handling of the F300 were more dependent than ever on the architecture under the skin. Although the F300 (and every Ferrari since) has been called a 'Rory Byrne Ferrari', the man himself is always quick to dismiss the phrase. "The whole thing is much bigger than that really, it's a true team effort," he said emphatically.

"I'm the chief designer but I don't really design the car. My function is to coordinate all the various research groups

Opposite, top: The furious outcry over Michael Schumacher's ill-judged attack on Jacques Villeneuve did not unsettle the Scuderia, which simply concentrated on getting it right for the following season. (Sutton)

Opposite, bottom: The 1998 F300 stands a good chance of being the most modified Formula One car in history. Everything was thrown at it in a bid to close the gap to Adrian Newey's stunning McLaren… including the extreme 'X-wings' here at Imola. (Shell/Getty Images)

– vehicle dynamics, structural calculation, detail design, aerodynamics… Really my main function is to coordinate all those various groups to give us the information to design the car. I'm probably responsible – give or take – for about 100 people involved in either design, research or other areas that support the design."

Although the F300 looked more compact than its predecessors, thanks to its aerodynamics, any advance was facilitated by Aldo Costa's structural architecture. For instance, a bigger, more bell-shaped fuel cell gave Brawn and the race team more flexibility in planning the race strategy, while also locating more of the weight of the fuel down around the centre of gravity height, to help in retrieving some of the handling lost to the regulations.

Opposite, left: A hive of industry, the Ferrari composites shop takes Rory Byrne's ideas and turns them into real, live racing cars that have won race after race. (Ferrari)

Opposite, right: With Ross Brawn coordinating them, the brilliant minds of Rory Byrne's chassis department and Paolo Martinelli's engine department unite into a formidable partnership. (Ferrari)

"Within my group, there are different groups that take care of the vehicle structure," said Costa. "Everything related to aerodynamics, electronics and engines comes outside my group – we concentrate on suspension, composites, chassis and the hydraulics systems. Rory is the chief designer, so technically he is my boss. So we work as a part of the design structure: we need to have on top one chief, and then we have the aerodynamics group, the vehicle dynamics group, the structural engineering group – all under the direction of Rory to make the design of the car."

Costa and his team really went to work on the suspension, rejecting the existing front assembly in its entirety. Barnard had packaged the front suspension with the dampers mounted horizontally along the top of the chassis, just in front of the cockpit, with the torsion bars mounted vertically on each side. This made for a compact, tidy arrangement that was easy to adjust on the grid or in the pits if the weather looked uncertain.

The arrangement had helped Schumacher to score victories such as the one Monaco in 1997 but, going into 1998, the team's focus was not on the eight Grands Prix it had won since Schumacher arrived, but rather on the 24 it had lost. By placing the dampers vertically in the nose, with the torsion bars mounted horizontally in front of them, there were immediate gains to be had in terms of grip at the cost of a little convenience. It seemed like a fair trade.

"There's an element of looking back at what worked in the past, but we try to optimise it," Byrne explained. "We haven't got infinite resources, and we can't do everything. The secret of a Formula One car is harnessing resources in the most efficient way. That means tackling the things that are going to give us performance, not expending resources on areas that might be nice, or where the technology might be interesting. The bottom-line is performance. If it doesn't give us performance for our investment, we just don't do it."

It is a measure of Byrne's confidence in the work of those around him that he was happy to go right to the limit with the F300, producing a car well below the minimum weight limit. This is a crucial attribute. It allows the required ballast to be placed strategically within the structure to achieve the optimum weight distribution.

With all the pieces in place, Ferrari packed up the new F300s and headed for Melbourne in mid-February 1998. This, surely, would be the moment when the years of upheaval and the massive investment that Jean Todt had instigated would be vindicated.

The Williams-Renault combine was no more. Ferrari had secured the best driver in the world, restructured the hallowed Gestione Sportiva and harnessed the formidable talents of Ross Brawn and Rory Byrne. Italy expected.

Unfortunately, nobody in Italy expected the resurgence of McLaren and Mercedes-Benz. Instead of a triumph in Melbourne, Ferrari was reduced to spectating as Mika Häkkinen and David Coulthard ran amok in an all-new Adrian Newey design, the MP4-13. They staged a formation 1-2 finish after lapping everyone else.

Brawn was philosophical about the blow. "You have to look at the situation and the circumstance," he said. "This is in no way an excuse, but Adrian had left Williams in February 1997 and was supposedly on 'gardening leave'. He was at a surprising number of races, though, as a McLaren

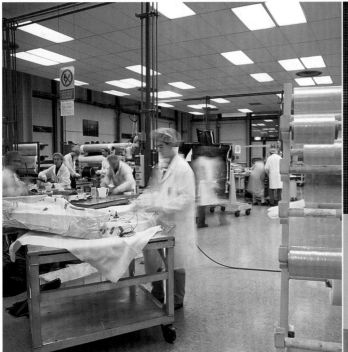

guest, for someone on 'gardening leave'. Adrian has a very fertile and creative mind. He spent much of 1997 creating a car without any of the distractions of racing one. Even if they were kept in his head, and not used until he set foot in the McLaren factory, it was natural that he should have had these thoughts and ideas, and put them to work the moment he arrived."

As well as Newey's MP4-13, McLaren had another ace up its sleeve in the form of Bridgestone. The Japanese tyre manufacturer had entered Formula One in 1997 and, despite not having a top team, put the likes of Prost Grand Prix on the podium from the outset. With Ferrari and Williams both still on Goodyear rubber, there was little surprise when McLaren jumped ship: it was a comfortable arrangement for Mercedes-Benz, whose AMG performance road car range had long enjoyed an exclusive supply of the Japanese tyres. By getting in with Bridgestone early, McLaren had been able to prepare for the new tyre regulations well in advance, and the new chassis had been developed together with Bridgestone's tyre compounds.

For his part, Brawn was full of admiration for a job well done – and then set about another season of aggressive pursuit. "We had to take a breath at the beginning of 1998, but we worked hard and, by the end of the year, we were back on terms again," he recalled.

The first target of Ferrari's fightback was its tyre supply. After the second race in Brazil, where Häkkinen and Coulthard finished a minute ahead of Schumacher, Goodyear responded to very public bullying and cajoling from Maranello in time for the third race in Argentina, by building new tyres specifically tailored to Ferrari's needs.

Meanwhile Byrne, Costa and the chassis team had launched a programme of development of a scale hitherto unseen even in Formula One. Through the course of 16 races, the F300 went through a total of seven different noses, four sidepod designs, five engine covers, three undertrays, six rear wings, two front suspension layouts, three rear suspension layouts, additional tower-mounted wings, a dorsal fin, any number of new flaps, fins, winglets

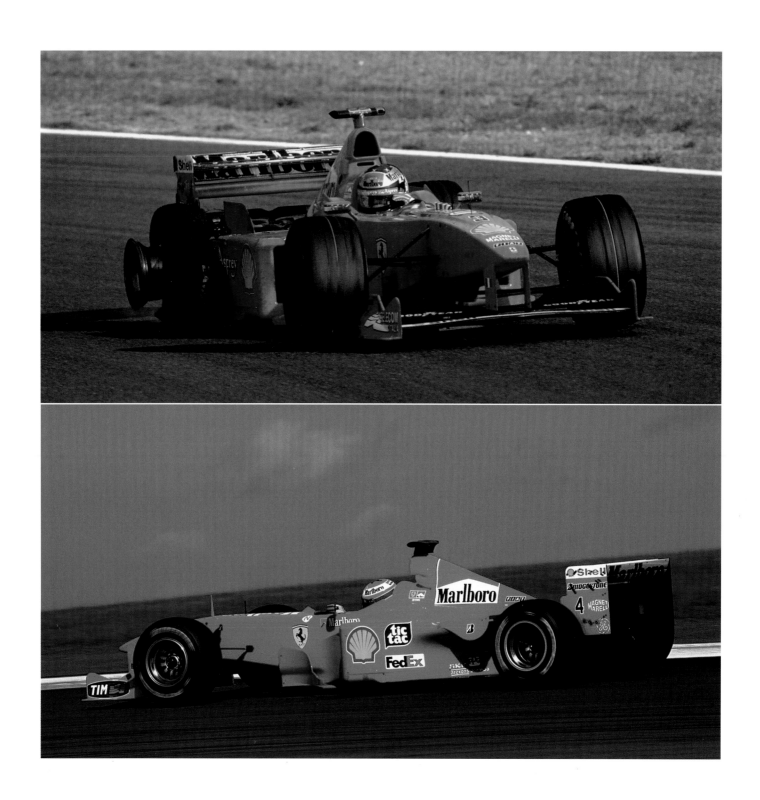

and vents, a revolutionary high-mounted exhaust system and, finally, a long-wheelbase specification.

It was an epic year's work that added six more wins to the Ferrari–Schumacher partnership prior to a month-long hiatus before the final round at Suzuka. The Gestione Sportiva was absolutely on the limit throughout this gap in the calendar, fitting in 17 days of testing in its efforts to close the four-point gap to Häkkinen. In Japan, Schumacher came out of the blocks to take pole position from his Finnish rival. The race, though, was a disaster: Schumacher stalled on the grid and later suffered a tyre blowout.

Two near-misses in two seasons…

The pace and scale of all the developments to the F300 made the development of the new 1999 car, the F399, a far less painful experience. So successful had been the push to get the front of the chassis handling properly that the development of the F399 was almost exclusively focused behind the cockpit. A new rear suspension layout mirrored that introduced at the front, and there was considerable development of the rear bodywork, undertrays and diffusers.

The main concern at the start of the season was the fact that Goodyear had withdrawn from Formula One, leaving Bridgestone with a monopoly. Now Ferrari was not merely without its bespoke rubber: it was also compelled to use tyres that had been specifically tailored to suit McLaren. Evidently Newey's team had developed a chassis that was benign on its rear tyres in 1998: but as soon as the Ferrari ran on the Bridgestones, it began consuming them with alarming speed.

Doubtless this was a legacy of the stiff suspension that Ferrari had adopted to pin the front of its cars to the road. Brawn, Byrne and Costa urgently shifted the focus of the technical team to overcome the problem.

More new regulations for 1999 required beefed-up rollover hoops, the addition of tethers to the wheels to stop them coming off in accidents, and development of the deformable structure at the back of the cars that would protect the driver from the shock of large rear impacts.

"For 1999, there weren't too many rule changes," Byrne remembered. "The Technical Regulations are pretty specific. They do go into an awful lot of detail and you are pretty limited in terms of scope generally."

Not that he was against testing the limits of the rules. In pre-season testing, the inherently unstable deformable rear-impact structure was used to mount the rear wing. At high speeds, the air passing over the wing would tip it back by around 3°, removing drag on the straights, thus making for a higher top speed. As the speed dropped off under braking for a corner, the wing would pop back up and the downforce would bite again. The FIA quickly banned the practice on the basis that this effectively constituted a moveable aerodynamic device, and also on safety grounds after Sauber's flexible wings broke in Brazil.

Nevertheless, rumours abounded to the effect that Ferrari's two-piece undertray was also flexible – that the aerodynamic venturi acted to suck the rear section down and thus massively to increase downforce. It was grist to the mill of Ferrari's main rivals at McLaren, especially when the F399 won first time out in Melbourne.

The winner was not Michael Schumacher, but his long-suffering sidekick Eddie Irvine, who was about to have the season of his life.

After winning in Australia, Irvine was right with Schumacher in the points table for the first half of the season, as Häkkinen and McLaren rallied and took the championship lead. The Ferrari pair were still behind Häkkinen coming into the British Grand Prix. Schumacher's season effectively ended in a crash on the opening lap.

The right rear brake of his F399 failed at the end of the long Hangar Straight after the bleed nipple had worked loose, sending him into the barriers – where a fractured suspension arm broke his right leg.

After three years as the number two, Irvine was left to take the fight to Häkkinen, aided by Schumacher's stand-in, Mika Salo. He won the next two races before a comparatively lean spell handed the initiative back to McLaren. At the European Grand Prix, almost unnoticed, Ferrari brought out new bargeboards to help clear the air

Opposite, top: A hundred thousand caps head for the bonfire: Michael Schumacher's 1998 World Championship bid was buried when his tyre let go in the last race at Suzuka. (Shell/Getty Images)

Opposite, bottom: Accidental heroes: Eddie Irvine and the Ferrari F399 were left to take the fight to McLaren in 1999 as Schumacher recuperated from his broken leg. (Shell/Getty Images)

more effectively beneath Irvine's title challenger, but inexplicably Irvine's pit crew lost his right rear wheel during his pitstop.

The next race was the penultimate Grand Prix in Malaysia, where Schumacher returned to his cockpit. The Ferraris filled the front row and Schumacher was insuperable before allowing Irvine through to win. Afterwards came a storm of controversy over those new bargeboards which, in post-race inspection, were found to be 5mm outside the permitted dimensions.

The words 'storm' and 'teacup' seemed applicable for what was widely agreed to have been a minimal infraction in an area of little significance. The team went back to the old bargeboards and undertray, but was unable to beat Häkkinen in Japan. Irvine missed out on the title by two points – but Ferrari was the Constructors' champion for the first time in 16 years.

Subsequently the problematical bargeboards from Sepang were declared eligible by the FIA Court of Appeal.

For 2000, Irvine was gone, and the fully repaired Schumacher was ready to take Scuderia Ferrari to the World Championship at the fifth time of asking. To this end, Byrne produced a car in the F1-2000 that clearly explained where the team's focus had been through 1999.

"Nowadays, from the time you start to the time you race a car, you're probably talking about a year," Byrne confirmed. "Of that order. We're always testing all sorts of things for next year. Certainly anything that's conceptually new or fundamentally new, we test. It might not mean the stuff we do at the circuit. It may just mean making some pieces and doing some tests on them to make sure that they're performing the way we expect them to perform."

No excuses and no oversights were permissible. The new car was another evolution of the original F300 concept – the devil being in the detail of what was, at first glance, a familiar package. "There were significant changes in the

Opposite: Stable of success – the prancing horses at rest between Grand Prix appearances in the Gestione Sportiva. (Ferrari)

Below: Flying start: armed with Byrne's F1-2000 Schumacher set a blistering pace early in the 2000 season to build a strong lead in the championship. (Shell/Getty Images)

rules for aerodynamics, the track and things like that," said Byrne. "So there was another step. But all the way through the designs have been an evolution, because that's how Formula One is these days."

The nose of the F1-2000 was even more steeply raked to squeeze more air through the undertray. The head protection was separated from the back of the cockpit to funnel air through to the rear wing, while the engine cover and the sidepods were cleaned up considerably, including McLaren-like 'chimneys' to divert hot, turbulent air away from the rear tyres and wing. All this added up to a 10% increase in aerodynamic efficiency. The title quest was also aided by increased sensitivity and adjustability in the front suspension design in ongoing development.

Schumacher got off to a flying start with the F1-2000. He won the first three races of the year while McLaren suffered hideous unreliability from Ilmor's latest Mercedes-Benz V10. Even when the MP4-15 hit its stride, Ferrari could rely on its in-built superiority in race strategy, courtesy both of the scrupulous advanced planning by Ross

Brawn, Luca Baldisserri and the race team, and of the flexibility offered by Aldo Costa's bottom-heavy fuel cell.

For all this, however, the championship almost slipped through Ferrari's hands during the mid-season races. The Ferrari management was embroiled in the 'battle of Bridgestone' that summer, attempting to wean the Japanese away from their symbiotic relationship with McLaren and into a long-term future at Maranello. The Bridgestones were still far better suited to Adrian Newey's designs, and Ferrari pushed as hard and as fast as it could to secure parity with its rivals.

"I think you need to analyse why it all went wrong, because we did have a 20-point lead," said Brawn. "There were four races where we scored very few points, and Häkkinen scored a lot of points – and then we were behind again. We had an engine failure at Magny-Cours, then we had two races where Michael was knocked

Byrne's F2001 would have to be pretty special to live up to its predecessor. The task of improving the package was again complicated by more rule changes from the FIA, which continued its battle against cornering speeds by raising the minimum height of the front wings by 5cm, and restricting the number and size of the rear wing elements. A further ban on the use of lightweight exotic materials in engine construction also created unwanted weight distribution problems.

The tried and tested centre section remained in place, with some detail improvements, but Byrne set about its extremities with a vengeance. The nose received yet another skyward tilt, but then swooped down hawkishly into a broad, flowing front wing.

This arrangement proved to be a very effective solution to the challenges imposed by the FIA. The F2001 proved itself to be every bit as fast as the previous year's car, out of the box. In fact, the ambitions of the governing body to slow down the cars were annulled when the new configuration greatly cleaned up of the airflow over the rest of the car. It was swiftly copied by everyone else in the paddock.

The team added new front brake housings that screened the mechanical parts inside aerodynamically shaped cases – something tried at Benetton back in the 1980s. Byrne was particularly pleased with a new one-piece front suspension set-up, which added rigidity and, more important, saved weight.

The combination of the new wing, brake and suspension designs reduced airflow disruption to a minimum and offered an appreciable saving in weight. It offset the disappointment of losing a novel rear wing design, buried in the rear suspension, which failed to make it past the FIA scrutineers early in the season.

Overall, however, the legality of the Ferrari and all the other cars was called into question on considerably fewer occasions in 2001, because the seven-year ban on 'driver-aid' software such as traction control was finally lifted. The former Benetton and later Ferrari electronics expert Tad Czapski was no longer with the team, but his influence was keenly felt in the arsenal of software built up over the

off in the first corner. Is there anything we could do to avoid that?"

Byrne, however, was not prepared to put this mid-season crisis down to bad luck. He was still preoccupied by the voracious appetite that his car was displaying for its Bridgestone tyres. He recalled: "By the time Belgium was finished, we understood what the problem was. We made some modifications which helped a bit, and then there was that really excellent effort from Michael at Monza."

Schumacher worked harder than ever to rescue the championship in that climactic Italian Grand Prix. Byrne was stunned by what he saw – even from a driver with whom he had worked for eight seasons. "That drive at Monza was really incredible," he said.

"So we got through 2000 and we obviously made the necessary design decisions for 2001. We knew we had a handle on the problem and that we could fix it, but really it meant designing a whole new car. That was what we did for 2001. It fundamentally solved the tyre problem."

The F2000 won all four of the season's closing races, so

Opposite: Straight-talking Ross Brawn demands nothing but perfection, and has seldom found the latest generation of Ferraris lacking. (Ferrari)

Above: Scuderia Ferrari Marlboro almost monopolised the top two steps on the podium in 2002 by virtue of the staggering pace and reliability of the F2002, which set new standards in Formula One. (Shell/Getty Images)

previous few seasons that led, from the fifth race of 2001, to the beginning of a new, licensed 'gizmo' era.

"When you have these constraints, there is a tendency for people to wonder exactly where the limit is, because sometimes it's very difficult to define," Brawn reflected. "If you've got the dimension of a rear wing, it's a dimension, end of story. It's almost black and white."

That word – 'almost' – is one of the keys to how Scuderia Ferrari Marlboro came to rewrite the history books. The relentless quest for perfection in the Gestione Sportiva allows no complacency in any area, no boundary to be left untested. The F2001 was the first car in which the technical team felt they had all the elements in place, and the results were devastating.

Opposite: The devil is in the detail in modern Formula One. The shark-like 'gills' in the sidepods of the F2003-GA are just one small, stylish part of the overall design. (Shell/Getty Images)

Ferrari's opposition was thoroughly demoralised by the F2001 by mid-season. McLaren fell away and Williams was fighting back slowly from its decline, its new BMW engines boasting Herculean power but inadequate reliability. Schumacher sealed his second successive championship in August, and ended the 2001 season with nine victories.

Williams welcomed Michelin back into the paddock to tackle the overwhelming superiority of Ferrari and Bridgestone and, in 2002, Ron Dennis's McLaren moved to join its "good friends and rivals" at Williams on Michelin tyres, leaving Bridgestone free to devote virtually all its attention to the Scuderia.

At the end of 2001, a new 'B' version of the F2001 had appeared, chassis 214, built in early October with radically different weight distribution. It had won in Japan before carrying out a full winter testing programme in readiness for the start of the following year's campaign. Not since the early 1980s had any team been able to run at the front with a year-old design but, and at the start of 2002, the F2001B was able to win in Australia and take third place in Malaysia. Meanwhile, back in Maranello, the final touches were being given to something really special.

The F2002 was unveiled at Maranello to a chorus of whispers about 'secret transmissions' – and still managed to produce a shock. The front end of the car was familiar but, at the back, all eyes were focused on how little of it there was.

Byrne: "The 2001 was the first of the cars with a low nose, then in 2002 we had a very low rear deck with a very low exhaust and radiator outlet arrangement that was quite different. The transmission was completely new, both in materials and concept, the cooling system was completely new, the way the chassis was constructed was new, the suspension and the way it was manufactured was new."

What the Gestione Sportiva chassis team did with the F2002 was create the perfect operational environment for the culmination of several years of work by the engine and transmission groups.

The tiny rear end was made possible by a cast titanium gearbox that had been developed in the back of Minardi Formula One cars since the start of 2000. Alternatives to the traditional cast magnesium or steel units had long been sought. Barnard had pioneered ventures into sheet titanium construction as far back as 1994, although the setbacks of the 1996 F310 were off-putting at the time. Other teams, notably Stewart-Ford in 1998, had attempted to make gearboxes completely from carbonfibre composites, but heat, vibration and lubrication problems had combined to make the idea unworkable.

Meanwhile Minardi, just down the road from Maranello, went to work on the titanium gearbox casing with metallurgy specialist CRP Technology in Modena. Not only did it offer a weight-saving of around 40% over anything that had come before, but it was 30% more rigid and 25% smaller.

This transmission was mated to the new 051 engine, which was designed to scale heights of up to 19,000rpm for the coming fight against BMW's standard-setting V10. Together the engine and gearbox provided the foundations of the chassis, with all efforts being made to focus on a centre of gravity height 23cm off the track surface. This meant that the radiators needed to be tipped forward in the sidepods, offering a larger cooling area while also significantly lowering the car's profile and reducing its wind resistance. This could only be achieved with a smaller fuel cell but, with the 'tyre war' between Bridgestone and

Michelin gathering pace, it was felt that most races would become two-stoppers by necessity.

Bridgestone would ensure that its tyres perfectly matched the F2002 all year, thanks in no small part to its own dedicated test team. Former Jaguar and Prost driver Luciano Burti would spend the season pounding round Fiorano, gathering data that allowed development of the compounds, construction and dimensions of the tyres. These would be honed to the unique needs of the F2002 – and further increase its performance advantage over the rest of the field.

Schumacher, having already established his championship lead with the interim F2001, had a lone F2002 at his disposal in Brazil. He won – and his season went into hyperspace. The opposition began to grumble privately about 'flexing' that was allegedly seen in the rear wing and bargeboards, although no official complaint was ever lodged.

Only one more race was lost all season. Schumacher never finished off the podium in a year that brought him 11 victories, and the fastest ever World Championship win (140 days). It made the F2002 the most dominant Ferrari Grand Prix car since the Formula Two 500 half a century before.

"The one that, for me, has been the most remarkable has been the 2002 car, because it really was the first car built entirely from the methodology of the technical group that we established," observed Aldo Costa happily. "But then in 2002, once the car was racing, for me the 2003 car became more important. Once the car is racing, it's time to start again and do a better design.

"We always do it like that. The best that you can do doesn't exist – any design can be improved. So all the time we work to improve. The 2002 car was a big step from the 2001 car, not because there was any weakness, but because we knew we could do better. So it goes with the 2003 car, and so on."

So it was that, when the F2003-GA appeared, it was another refinement on the previous year's car. Once again, the main advance was beneath the skin, namely Gilles Simon's revolutionary 052 engine. Its increased cylinder bore diameter made it longer than the 051 and demanded a fractionally longer wheelbase, and another reduction in the fuel cell volume. Byrne meanwhile entertained himself by smoothing and integrating the lines of the F2003-GA and

making the lip where the undertray meets the sidepods more pronounced, effectively fitting the car with a miniature version of the twin-floor setup of the unloved F92A.

When the new car made its race debut in Spain the result was, at first sight, emphatic. The front row of the grid was all red and there were two happy drivers on the podium. Schumacher took his second successive victory to close in on the impudent Kimi Räikkönen's early season lead, while Barrichello took third place with his third podium finish of the season and set the fastest lap of the race.

Yet the people most encouraged by the new Ferrari's performance were dressed in anything but red. Barcelona offered a circuit that flattered the F2003-GA's greatest strengths – straight-line speed and stupendous grip in medium and high-speed corners – and yet Michael Schumacher had been harried to the flag by Fernando Alonso's underpowered Renault, which was mighty through the sinewy middle sector of the lap.

McLaren, Williams and Renault all saw that the new car did not embody the great leap in performance that they had

expected. Their fear of the unknown dissolved even as the champagne was being sprayed in Barcelona... the new Ferrari was good, but there was little evidence of the great strides shown over the F2002 in testing.

Behind closed doors in Maranello a long, hard campaign and many sleepless nights appeared to be in prospect as it became clear that the FIA's regulation changes had undone so much of the planning that had gone into the new car. Single-lap qualifying, with its back-to-front order on Friday and teams being forced to run Saturday's session in race trim, had wrought havoc on the philosophy of the F2003-GA.

Right: Young Brazilian star Felipe Massa had a busy year in 2003 pounding round the test tracks trying to tune the F2003-GA's handling to match the Michelin cars. (Ferrari)

If the F2002 had suffered a weak spot, it was in qualifying trim. As the previous season progressed, the king of qualifying had been Juan Pablo Montoya in the long-wheelbase Williams FW24, a car that was noticeably kinder on its front tyres in qualifying trim than was the Ferrari.

Opposite: Ultimately, the determination of Michael Schumacher just kept the F2003-GA ahead of the field to claim both championships – although it remains an extremely successful F1 car. (Ferrari)

Working on the assumption that Williams and McLaren would up their game in race trim, it became imperative to make sure that the new Ferrari could start on the front row and a longer chassis, following the FW24 philosophy, was adopted. Unlike the long-wheelbase F310B of 1997, however, the new car wasn't stretched to shuffle the driver, fuel tank and engine forward to tip the balance onto the front wheels. Within the F2003-GA's longer chassis the cockpit was further back, pushing the longer, more slender engine and fuel tank back in turn, and moving the weight towards the rear axle.

Thus the new car was designed to be kinder to its front tyres in qualifying. Under the 2002 regulations it could then be trimmed out overnight using aerodynamics and ballast to give a more nose-heavy set-up for the race... but then came Max Mosley's 'February revolution', and Ferrari found itself on it's back foot.

Ironically, the technical package of the year was the Williams-BMW FW25 – a car that had been designed with the dominance of the Ferrari F2002 very much in the minds of its creators. Amongst the BMW and Williams wizardry it featured the spoon-shaped front wing, tiny titanium gearbox and short-wheelbase set-up first seen on the all-conquering Ferrari.

The dock-tailed Williams proved to be an enigma in the early races, and the team struggled to understand the new car's behaviour. It was Monaco before a change of suspension geometry and a new compound of Michelin tyre finally set the team's 2003 season alight. Thereafter the FW25 presided over the other cars in the field, perfectly suited to the new format of the race weekend, comfortably faster than the venerable McLaren MP4/17 and a Ferrari that could not be optimised for qualifying or the race.

Within the Gestione Sportiva there was considerable frustration, but no panic. Williams lacked two crucial components – the Rolling Stones-like durability of Ferrari's V10 engines, and a lead driver of Michael Schumacher's ability and standing to galvanise the team.

The Anglo-German team gave away points with gay abandon, through a combination of engine maladies, unforced errors and the ongoing battle between its two drivers. The threat from McLaren of an all-new MP4/18 did not materialise – the radical Adrian Newey car proving too frail to ever turn a wheel in anger – while the progress of the Renault team towards the front of the grid only served

to take points away from Ferrari's rivals, limiting the damage to its 2003 campaign.

Before the British Grand Prix in July the Gestione Sportiva put in a momentous programme of testing, running new aerodynamics aimed at trying to reduce the fundamental tail-heaviness of the F2003-GA. The British race aside, where interruptions, weather and an inspired Rubens Barrichello brought about the most popular victory of the year, those improvements weren't good enough. Schumacher limped home seventh and a lap down in Germany, then eighth and a lap down in Hungary, to give him a Driver's Championship standing just one point ahead of Juan Pablo Montoya, himself just a point clear of Kimi Räikkönen, with three races to go.

Prior to the Gran Premio d'Italia, Ferrari mobilised as never before, testing the latest engine, aerodynamic and tyre developments to breaking point. In three days of preparation at Monza, the squad of Schumacher, Barrichello, Luca Badoer and Felipe Massa put in 649 laps, while simultaneously Massa, Badoer and a recalled Luciano Burti put in almost 500 more laps at Fiorano. The result was three wins, two pole positions and two fastest laps to seal the eighth and ninth titles out of ten available in Ferrari's dominant spell since 1999.

The F2003-GA will not go down in history as one of the greatest Formula One cars, even though in Rory Byrne's estimation it remains 'the best Ferrari of all time.' In truth it's only failing was in following on from the dazzling F2002. Yet this was a car that won seven of the twelve races it contested in 2003 – a strike rate almost 20% higher than the seminal Lotus 49 in its championship-winning year of 1968. On reflection, the previous winter's confidence was well founded.

Chapter Six

THE FERRARI DRIVER

An image of a man taking on the best cars and drivers in the world, pitting his skill and bravery against his mortality to uphold the honour of the scarlet cars, is the fantasy of every man, woman and child in Italy. It is yet another part of the legend nurtured by Enzo Ferrari.

"As far as I'm concerned, there has only been one truly great racing driver," he said. "There is a perfect balance between a car and its driver – 50% car and 50% driver. With Nuvolari, this relationship was overturned. He contributed at least 75% of the total."

Tazio Nuvolari, the 'Flying Mantuan', drove for Ferrari from 1933 until 1937, and cast a long shadow from which few of the Scuderia's subsequent drivers have fully emerged. His was often a fruitless task, for the Alfa Romeos that Ferrari campaigned were simply of another, altogether gentler time than the awesome Mercedes-Benz and Auto Union 'Silver Arrows'... although Nuvolari never once let that fact get the better of him.

He would race come what may, turning out with his leg in plaster, once even a full body cast. And he would never stint from the full-blooded four-wheel-drifting style with which he attacked every corner.

His finest hour came in 1935, when he raced an Alfa Romeo P3 to an astonishing victory in the German Grand Prix at the Nürburgring, watched by a furious Nazi propaganda minister, Josef Goebbels. So confident had been the Germans of winning their home race that they had not bothered to bring a gramophone record of anything except

Master of all he surveys: Michael Schumacher has stood out over the rest of the stars in Formula One for almost a decade. (Getty Images/Clive Mason)

Deutschland über alles. Even as the Nazis were engaged on a difficult telephone call to their Führer, so the story goes, Nuvolari quietly handed an official a recording of *La Marcia Reale* from his briefcase (see Chapter 8).

Nuvolari's last hurrah came at the wheel of one of Ferrari's first creations, the Tipo 166, in the 1948 Mille Miglia. Although wracked by the lung disease that would eventually kill him, Nuvolari took the Ferrari by the scruff of the neck and raced it until it literally fell apart. When he took the lead, one mudguard was gone, as was the bonnet. His seat fell off, the rear brakes gave up, and still he led right into the closing stages. Then one pothole too many demolished the remains of the car's suspension, and it was all over. Soon Nuvolari himself was in terminal decline, lamenting: "I no longer count for anything in the world."

In fact, the example that Nuvolari set remained the benchmark for everyone who drove for Ferrari. It took over a quarter of a century for anyone to come close to Nuvolari's blueprint of the perfect racing driver, as Ferrari himself admitted: "When they presented me with this tiny Canadian, this miniscule bundle of nerves, I instantly recognised in him the physique of the great Nuvolari. And I said to myself: 'Let's give him a try.'"

That man was Gilles Villeneuve, whose bewitching of the *Ingegnere*, of the Gestione Sportiva and of motor racing as a whole would last four-and-a-half tumultuous seasons from the end of 1977. But if his career drew comparison with Nuvolari's, it was because Scuderia Ferrari was almost completely incapable of giving him a competitive car.

Watching at home on TV, the Old Man would laugh out loud with delight at Villeneuve's antics, such as his famous, wheel-banging battle in the 1979 French Grand Prix with the Renault of René Arnoux. The crashes were many, but Ferrari merely labelled his prodigy 'the high priest of destruction' and ordered the Gestione to build stronger cars.

In 1982, Ferrari finally produced, in its 126C2, a car capable of giving Villeneuve a World Championship. Mauro Forghieri's turbocharged V6 was hugely powerful and married to a state-of-the-art chassis from Harvey Postlethwaite.

But, in qualifying at Zolder for the Belgian Grand Prix, Villeneuve was killed, leaving Ferrari distraught. "My past is scarred with grief," he said. "Father, mother, brother, son, wife... my life is full of sad memories. I look back and I see my loved ones, and among my loved ones I see the face of this great man, Gilles Villeneuve."

Ferrari never wanted for superb drivers in Villeneuve's wake: Didier Pironi, Michele Alboreto, Nigel Mansell, Alain Prost, Gerhard Berger. But the superiority of the British teams, Williams and McLaren, added to the political maëlstrom of Maranello, left success – never mind domination – a distant ambition.

Throughout Ferrari's darkest days, there was one shaft of light to which the tifosi clung, in the form of Jean Alesi. His arrival in Formula One with Tyrrell had been sensational. He had finished fourth on his debut in the 1989 French Grand Prix, diced for the lead with Ayrton Senna in the 1990 US Grand Prix, and speared the revolutionary,

high-nosed Tyrrell 019 into the top three on a regular basis through the remainder of the season.

The world was Alesi's oyster, and he signed an option to go to Williams in 1991 – a piece of paper might have brought him all the dominance of the Adrian Newey and Renault years of 1991–97. Yet, although the banns were effectively read out, the marriage was not to be: the French-Sicilian was wooed away by Ferrari, after Ayrton Senna had rejected the Scuderia's advances.

To watch Alesi wrestling the brutish, twin-floored 1992 car, for instance, was often awe-inspiring. In the French Grand Prix, he stayed out on slicks during a downpour, and the gamble almost paid off – until the F92A hurled itself off the road at 170mph for no apparent reason, logging the biggest spin that Ferrari data-acquisition systems had ever recorded.

Opposite: Jean Alesi struck sparks wherever he went, and was the last of the old-school drivers whose pride and passion were obvious to his devoted fans. (LAT)

Enzo Ferrari would doubtless have been delighted but, in the cold, hard world of Formula One, it was merely taken as proof that the old days were in the past.

Into the role of *direttore sportivo* came Jean Todt, and again Ferrari tried to woo Ayrton Senna into the fold. Senna felt he would be 'incomplete' without stirring the passions evoked by Ferrari but, despite having the financial might of Marlboro at his bidding, the pragmatist in him won out. The great Brazilian went to Williams – with the intention of joining Ferrari for 1996.

Todt, meanwhile, retained Alesi and Berger, whose popularity continued to rise outside the team – if not always inside it. "They were part of the team," Todt reflected with generosity. "I would say that all drivers have to get something from the team before they can deliver something back. At that time, they were getting a poor service from Ferrari. The cars they were driving were not very competitive, not very reliable.

"So: they were there, they were patient, but they were nervous because they weren't getting what they had been expecting. That was the major problem. We had no right to expect a lot from them."

Solitary wins for Berger in 1994 and Alesi in 1995 were small comfort for the Scuderia, and tempers began to fray. Todt demanded nothing but the best for the team in 1996

and, with Senna dead, that meant hiring Michael Schumacher – much to the chagrin of the incumbents.

"Alesi has been very clear," said Ferrari president Luca di Montezemolo. "He has said that Schumacher's presence is not compatible with him. Alesi knows how much I admire him. But I have told him this and I say it again: it is important not to make accusations about treachery – and not to behave like a little baby."

So the Alesi–Berger era simply fizzled out. They decamped together somewhat huffily to Benetton, while Todt, Ferrari, Marlboro and Shell looked forward to a bright new era, with V10 power and Michael Schumacher at the wheel.

"You can't really judge a driver when the successful qualities in the car don't exist," says Todt today. "We knew that, if we gave Michael the cars they [Berger and Alesi] had had, he would not win races. You can't expect a driver to change everything. He can be the point of reference for a team, but first you need to give to him, before you can expect to get from him."

How different an epitaph will there be for Michael Schumacher's time at Maranello? If today's Scuderia Ferrari Marlboro, formed around its star of today, is very different to the team he joined at the end of 1995, so too is the man himself a very different sort of Ferrari driver. It is one of Schumacher's greatest achievements that he has finally broken the legacy of Nuvolari, and dragged Ferrari into a new age of hero.

Being number one in the team is one thing. Getting the team to be 'number one' is entirely another, but this is how Schumacher excelled, long before the glory days arrived.

Luca Baldisserri is the man who tended Schumacher's cars day-in, day-out on their way to three consecutive World Championships. His impression is that here is a driver for whom any team would cheerfully commit murder – a *racing* driver, who is right on the button from the start of free practice.

"When Michael goes out first-thing, if the track is 'green', he is always fast – often fastest," Baldisserri said. "That's 70% him and 30% preparation. He has that commitment, but we know already that he's on the ball, so we're not very impressed. We know he's quite quick! If, on the other hand, he's not so quick, we know we have a problem…"

It is impossible to overestimate the importance of such confidence in the man at the wheel. So many drivers, be they great, good or indifferent, have failed to provide a barometer like this, but Schumacher has, and throughout his career. His application is there in spades and, if there is a problem with a car, he will analyse it, rather than simply drive through it. Likewise his 'off-days' can be counted on the fingers of one hand. There is rarely a trough in the reserves that he has within himself.

To the Gestione Sportiva engineers, moved neither by Schumacher's promotional appeal nor by the wages of risk that inflate a Formula One driver's salary, this means that he is worth every penny: he helps the engineers to create the best racing cars in the world. Paolo Martinelli, the technical director of the Formula One engine programme: "There are areas where the driver has to support [the team] in terms of judgement, in terms of priority. Michael is very clear-minded in his support of the engineering, in giving us priorities for development, in judging the characteristics of a new engine.

Above: It was one of the most popular partnerships in Ferrari's history, but Jean Alesi and Gerhard Berger too often ended their races in disappointment, as here in Monaco in 1995. Soon Ferrari announced the arrival of Michael Schumacher. (LAT)

Opposite, top: Fiat patriarch Gianni Agnelli said that, if Schumacher did not win, the Ferrari team would be to blame. Victories were hard to come by in 1996, and soon Ross Brawn and Rory Byrne were summoned to Maranello. (Shell/Getty Images)

Opposite, bottom: Just after the terrorist attacks on the USA in September 2001, a preoccupied Michael Schumacher had one of his rare off-days in the Italian Grand Prix. (Shell/Getty Images)

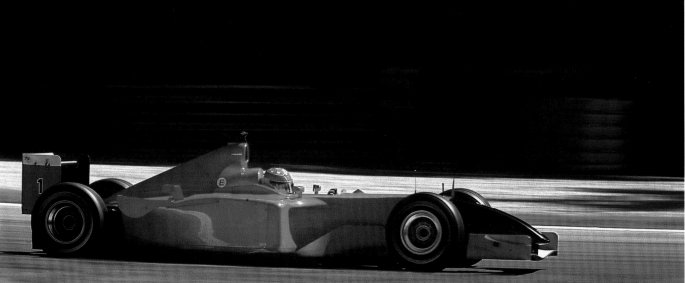

"Of course, when you have a good product, you have positive feelings, but there can also be negative points that must be improved. You have to focus on fixing these points. That is where the activity of the driver, of Michael, is fundamental."

Martinelli's V10 programme, under the design direction of Gilles Simon, was already well advanced by the time that Schumacher arrived. The chassis engineering team has had greater cause to thank him, for it was Schumacher who initiated the fundamental rethink that led to the arrival of his former colleagues at Benetton, Ross Brawn and Rory Byrne, to take command of the technical team.

Although Schumacher was doubtless buoyed by their arrival, he had insisted on reuniting the team that had delivered his 1994–95 titles for reasons of altogether greater importance than simply rekindling the *camaraderie* at Benetton. The F310 and F310B with which he began his Ferrari career were products of John Barnard's mind. Barnard's school of thinking was steeped in success, but it was also fundamentally at odds with Schumacher's.

"For sure, Michael was completely new for us in terms of driving style," said Luca Baldisserri. "He likes the car [balanced] more to the front, because he's not worried about a 'light' car in the entry of the corner. And he gives us a big advantage with new things like traction control: if we want to identify a problem, he helps us because he likes to fight with the traction of the car.

"When Michael came, we not only changed the way we set up our cars. We changed the way we *designed* the cars. If you make a mistake on the set-up, the car will be slow – if you do a perfect set-up, the car will be at the performance you desire. But you can't do a good set-up if the car is no good for the driver. So Michael has taken the design a certain way."

That 'certain way' was the product of Schumacher's schooling at Benetton under Brawn's watchful eye, in cars designed by Byrne. In fact, of everyone in Formula One, Byrne may be the best-placed to settle any debate over comparisons between Michael Schumacher and Ayrton Senna. He has worked with both drivers at the start of their Formula One careers, Senna at Toleman in 1984 after he had only had three Formula One test sessions, and Schumacher at Benetton after one Grand Prix, with Jordan. Yet this is the one subject on which the affable South African shows any sign of agitation (see sidebar).

Byrne: "I've also worked with Nelson Piquet, who was towards the end of his career, but all three were multiple World Champions and all three have exhibited the same characteristic: the capacity to process things quickly even while driving quickly."

After a dozen years of working together, there are still things that Schumacher can do to surprise and delight those around him, as Byrne readily testified: "Michael can be on a qualifying lap and still have time to talk on the radio if he has to, and it won't affect his lap-time or anything. There are very few drivers who can do that. The World Champions I've worked with could.

"It's their *speed*, their ability to process things in their minds even while doing the basic job of driving better than anyone else. And it's their total dedication – that's the other thing. They have 100% dedication to the job and the expectation of nothing less than that from everyone else around them."

Byrne's introduction to the man who would make his cars great was accidental. Like many in Formula One, he was taken by complete surprise at the 1991 Belgian Grand Prix, when an unknown youngster in an under-funded Jordan appeared fourth on the timesheets in free practice, in the thick of the elite formed by Williams, McLaren, Benetton and Ferrari, solidly among names like Senna, Prost, Mansell and Piquet.

Back then, Eddie Jordan was in his first year as a constructor and, while his bright green cars were stealing points with aplomb, they were not able to balance his books. Moreover one of his drivers, Bertrand Gachot, had been imprisoned before the race for assaulting a London taxi driver with mace spray. Into the breach came Schumacher's manager, Willi Weber, who offered Jordan a replacement driver – and a little help with his accounting difficulties.

Give the boy a chance, said Weber, and Mercedes-Benz

will be pleased to pay for his ride. Jordan, the self-styled talent-spotter, was interested, but only if Schumacher had some experience of Spa-Francorchamps. Weber was somewhat economical with the truth at this point, and sent Schumacher off on a bicycle while the deal was finalised.

Looking back from a decade later, as Schumacher took his 52nd Grand Prix victory with another scintillating drive around Spa, Jordan remembered the deal fondly. "That morning the bailiffs had locked up the truck because I had no money, and they claimed that I owed money to somebody – which was a complete fallacy, of course," he laughed. "We needed a few quid from Mercedes and, God bless 'em, they paid."

As his major benefactor, Mercedes-Benz had been grooming Michael Schumacher for some time. The combination of his skill at the wheel and Willi Weber's adroitness as a personal manager had brought Stuttgart funding for the greater part of Schumacher's career. First, he had been taken from Formula Three into a coveted slot in the Mercedes-Benz Junior Team, alongside his peers Heinz-Harald Frentzen and Karl Wendlinger.

This was a bid by Mercedes to right one of the greatest wrongs in the history of the World Championship, and produce the first-ever German World Champion. After the heydays of Rudi Caracciola, Bernd Rosemeyer and Hermann Lang as European champions before the war, the Fatherland had endured a lean time. Wolfgang von Trips had come heartbreakingly close for Ferrari in 1961, only to be killed in the Italian Grand Prix. In the 1980s, Stefan Bellof had been arguably the find of the decade until a horrible crash in a sportscar race at Spa had ended his life, too.

So the Mercedes-Benz Motorsport management – Jochen Neerpasch, PR man Norbert Haug, technical director Hermann Hiereth and team manager Max Welti – had picked three likely lads. In his first season of Formula Three in 1989, with the WTS team's Reynard-VW, Schumacher had been beaten by a single point to the German title by Wendlinger, tying in second place with Frentzen – before going on to win the 1990 championship.

That same season and through 1991, Schumacher had perfected the art of racing a 5-litre turbocharged Group C sportscar, as had his young colleagues. The Sauber-

Mercedes were mighty cars to master, but all three did, under the tutelage of former Formula One driver Jochen Mass. They were also educated in the art of handling the media and every other aspect of life as sporting superstars – for it was clear that all three had the potential.

For Schumacher, the potential was realised with Jordan at Spa – the ultimate 'driver's circuit'. He had never raced there, but he qualified seventh, and snatched sixth place off the start.

But his race went little further: the Jordan's clutch failed within half a lap, leaving him stranded to watch the race being won by Ayrton Senna's McLaren. "I guarantee you there's nobody who knows too much about what's happening in sports car racing at the moment," remembered Eddie Jordan of his own shock at Schumacher's pace. "It was no different then."

One thing that was different then, however, was that Ross Brawn had been newly installed as the technical director at Benetton after his boss, Tom Walkinshaw, had bought into the team. Through the opening two-thirds of that season, Brawn had been guiding his TWR-built Jaguar XJR-14 to victory in the World Sportscar Championship – at the same time keeping a very close eye on a certain youngster at Sauber-Mercedes.

"It was blindingly obvious that this was a major talent," recalled Brawn. "Mercedes had this very democratic process where each car had two or three drivers and they did the same number of laps. Mercedes was into driver training so Michael would get a one-half or a one-third share of the car in each race. We used to dread it when he got in the car because we knew he was going to give us a hard time…

"Frentzen and Wendlinger couldn't match him, and in a number of ways. They couldn't match him in fuel consumption, they couldn't match him in pace. He was very clearly a star when we first saw him in sports cars."

Just after Schumacher's stunning debut for his team, Eddie Jordan received another big cheque from Mercedes-Benz – this time in compensation. The irreverent Irishman

and his happy band were good at making headlines, but clearly somebody had felt that the *wunderkind* needed some firmer ground on which to establish himself. The next race was the Italian Grand Prix at Monza and, rather than the green driving suit of Jordan, Schumacher appeared wearing the yellow overalls of Benetton – with a contract that would take him to the end of 1995.

This was the result of very slick work by Walkinshaw and Brawn. "He was tied down to a Mercedes contract so, when we started in Formula One, we never thought that Michael would be that available," Brawn said. "But what happened, I *think*, was that Mercedes and Willi Weber decided they wanted him to have a go in Formula One. Lo and behold, he turned up in a Jordan. We knew long before that how good he was. So Tom persuaded Flavio Briatore to put maximum effort into getting him to Benetton."

Alerted by the no-show of Schumacher and his management at a planned contract signing, Eddie Jordan sought an injunction to stop Benetton 'stealing' his man. This

was refused. "I will not take any money," Jordan raged at the time. "There's a thing called principle! They won't buy me!"

The Benetton team, under the stewardship of Briatore and Walkinshaw, said that it had all been above board. The governing body declared that it was 'matter of conscience'. But Jordan raged on until a paternal word from McLaren boss Ron Dennis, who simply told him: "Welcome to the Piranha Club." The nickname for the Formula One paddock lives on to this day.

Moreno was handed half a million dollars by Benetton and Mercedes-Benz, and took the vacant seat at Jordan for the rest of the season. In a more sanguine mood, a decade later, at Spa, Jordan grinned: "I gave Michael his chance, and he buzzed off afterwards, and we got a few more quid, and we're still friends."

Keeping his friends is a Michael Schumacher speciality – not least among them Norbert Haug, now the director of Mercedes-Benz Motorsport. When Schumacher next came to contract negotiations, it was the summer of 1995, and many assumed that he and his mentors at Mercedes would

be reunited at McLaren, which had taken over from Sauber as the works-supported team.

It was assumed that it had always been the intention of the Stuttgart firm that Schumacher would spearhead its first Formula One title bid in 40 years. Of the Junior Team trio, Wendlinger had never fully got back onto Formula One pace after an enormous shunt at Monaco in 1994 had put him in a coma, while Frentzen was doing well enough at Sauber. Schumacher, though, was now a double World Champion and the darling of Germany. Anywhere he went, Shell and Philip Morris were likely to go, too – and, for the time being, they were at Marlboro McLaren Mercedes.

Certainly, McLaren's Ron Dennis was keen. While Senna had been holding out for a Williams-Renault in 1993, overtures had been made towards Schumacher, and now it seemed that nothing could stop them getting their man. All through that summer, the interested parties – Williams included – drew up their plans. But Ferrari was ahead of them all.

"We were looking at the other drivers, but definitely the reference was Michael," said Jean Todt of that remarkable

summer. "After the first meetings with Willi Weber, the next step was to meet Michael. Weber, our lawyer, myself and he all met in Monte Carlo in August 1995, just the four of us, and we had a meeting which lasted for 12 hours. When we finished the meeting, he had signed the contract."

That contract was the most lucrative in the history of world motorsport – worth $24 million a year for two years. Todt: "During the meeting, just to get agreement, I had various phone calls with Montezemolo, but they were the only people involved. I have read a lot of things saying that Bernie was central to it, but it was I who called Bernie just before we told the press that Michael had signed with us."

The reaction in the pit-lane at the Hungaroring, where the deal was announced, was one of shock. "I really don't understand him," said Renault engine project leader Bernard Dudot. "We've proved yet again that our engines are the best, and the Ferraris finish a lap behind – when they finish! With us, he could have won the championship again. I just don't get it."

Schumacher, too, appeared somewhat bewildered by it all. "When I started to race in cars, I didn't know much about Formula One or Ferrari," he said. "I'd arrived in motorsport very quickly but, ever since I was young, all I'd known was that Ferrari is a big part of Formula One, but I didn't understand why. I'm sure I'll appreciate the situation more and more in the coming years."

One can only assume that, at Mercedes-Benz, Haug *did* appreciate the situation, for he took Schumacher's defection on the chin. Indeed when, five years later, Schumacher finally claimed the World Championship for Ferrari, it was with Haug that Schumacher was spotted partying (in a 'Portakabin'). Several surprised Formula One people were amazed to see such hearty roister-doistering, such trading of insults over beers and cigars, while the Ferrari team packed up ready for the next race. But clearly Haug's disappointment for McLaren-Mercedes was tempered by the end of Schumacher's long wait.

Although Schumacher retains an affection for his compatriots at Mercedes, the years of working towards and creating a new 'Ferrari era' changed his life forever. "He's a very important part of the team, there's no doubt about it, and he's very much part of the 'family'," said Ross Brawn,

Above: Charity work and football are two of the mainstays of life for Michael Schumacher outside the cockpit – happily for him, they often coincide. (Shell/Getty Images)

Opposite: Luca Baldisserri watched over the cars of Eddie Irvine throughout his Ferrari career, and was disappointed not to have won both the Drivers'

and Constructors' championships in 1999. (Shell/Getty Images)

"It's almost a unique position in Formula One. I'm not sure any other driver has become as closely integrated with a team as he has with Ferrari. I can't imagine him really wanting to drive anywhere else."

Such is the strength of Schumacher's grip at Ferrari that driving for the Scuderia is no longer every racer's dream but, for some, the worst kind of nightmare. For his number two, life in Schumacher's shadow is never dull, but often fruitless.

Almost as soon as he arrived in Formula One, Schumacher's ability to send his team mates hastening for the door has been a hallmark. In 1991, five races alongside Nelson Piquet at Benetton were enough to send the triple World Champion into retirement. The following year, Tom Walkinshaw partnered him with his own favourite, Martin Brundle, who just avoided the chop at the mid-season point, such was the gulf between them. Then followed Riccardo Patrese, JJ Lehto and Jos Verstappen through the next two seasons.

At the start of 1995, the cheeky British driver Johnny Herbert outpaced his new Benetton team mate in pre-season testing. It proved to be a bad move on his part: he found his track-time somewhat limited thereafter.

Small wonder that, for 1996, it was hard work for Jean Todt to find anyone willing to race not alongside his new star, but a respectful couple of paces behind. Gerhard Berger was seen as the ideal man, but he had too much pride – and too high a market value – and quit Ferrari for Benetton. David Coulthard had potential, but he signed up for McLaren in the belief that, alongside Mika Häkkinen, his status as a race winner would guarantee equal status.

Nicola Larini and Luca Badoer both had perfect CVs, but asking an Italian to play second fiddle to a German in the national team would be unthinkable...

Then one day Ferrari president Luca di Montezemolo was accosted in the paddock by Jordan's roguish driver Eddie Irvine, who demanded that he should be given a discount on spares for his 288 GTO road car. From little acorns, great partnerships are sometimes formed.

Irvine was under no illusions about what he was expected to do. He was Schumacher's wingman, no more and no less – a role none but the unswervingly self-confident would accept. He was also given one of the best

race engineers in the business in the shape of Luca Baldisseri, who was a calming influence on many occasions.

"It was very difficult for Eddie and, I have to say, for me as well," said Baldisserri. "You can imagine: Michael was twice World Champion when he came to Ferrari, and it was very exciting to have him here. We had to prove to him that Ferrari could provide success. So I have to say that all the team was working for Michael – there was not a lot of room for a second driver at that stage in 1996."

Irvine's value, however, was much in evidence in 1997. As the title-winning trio of Schumacher, Brawn and Byrne reunited around the disappointing F310B chassis, Irvine led Ferrari's attack on Jacques Villeneuve and Williams-Renault. He taunted and cajoled Villeneuve through the media, knocked him off the road, generally made life as miserable as possible for the Canadian, while the team honed the car to Schumacher's liking. In a defining moment, Irvine shot round the outside of everyone through the sweeping S-bends of his beloved Suzuka, on a light fuel load, and wore the Williams into the ground before moving

Left: Under fire from all sides, the post-Silverstone 1999 pairing of Eddie Irvine and Mika Salo won races and dodged conspiracy theories, but fell short of World Championship success.
(Shell/Getty Images)

Below: Scuderia Ferrari Marlboro has worked hard in support of Rubens Barrichello, who has often borne the brunt of its misfortune.
(Ferrari)

over for Schumacher. "Waiting for the phone call," he called it.

But it was Irvine, not Schumacher, who very nearly won the 1999 World Championship. "Michael broke his leg and, in my heart, I thought that was the first year we could have won it," said Brawn. "Eddie did almost win the championship, and took it down to the last race. No disrespect to him, but I have the feeling that, if Michael had been around, there might have been a different result."

With Schumacher on the sidelines, Irvine's place as number two was filled by Finnish driver Mika Salo. In sharp contrast with his compatriot and bitter rival Mika Häkkinen, Salo had seldom been given a chance to shine since being narrowly beaten by 'the quicker Mika' in the 1990 British Formula Three championship. He began quietly, trailing in ninth place behind a victorious Irvine in Austria, but then made a bid for glory in Germany.

He beat Irvine to fourth on the grid and rocketed through to second place at the start, chasing Häkkinen. The McLaren was delayed by a refuelling rig failure, letting Salo through to lead. Irvine took advantage of the misfortune of others to climb from sixth place on the first lap to second in the closing stages, at which point the team ordered Salo to move aside. Which he did, driving in Irvine's wheeltracks to the end.

The Italian press went ape. What, they wondered, was the point of shovelling millions of dollars in Schumacher's direction, if Salo could do just as good a job? And what was the point in Irvine winning if not on merit?

Oddly enough, Salo's performance fell away at the next round in Hungary. There were whispers – starting not far from the Finn – that he had been slipped a full fuel load in qualifying.

This situation effectively left Irvine on his own against the McLarens, and he ultimately failed to get the job done. At the end of the year, both were gone, Irvine to Jaguar (to become the highest-paid employee of Ford Motor Company), Salo back to the shallow water at Sauber.

It was an unfortunate season all round, and marked the end of Baldisserri's time with Irvine. "I don't think he was able to work as the first driver," he said simply. "He had these things in his mind that he was always

under Michael and, psychologically, it was completely different when he had to do the job. When you have to work at the top, you need a completely different mentality to drive yourself and the team, and I don't think Eddie was ready for that. Ultimately our weakness in 1999 was Eddie himself."

At the 2000 Spanish Grand Prix, Brawn made a contentious statement: "Rubens Barrichello has done more for Ferrari in four races than Eddie Irvine did in four years."

Four seasons later, Brawn's respect for Irvine's replacement has grown further. "Rubens has become a very important member of the team," he said. "As each season goes on, he's getting closer to the team – even though he has always had the difficulty of coming along after Michael. I think the environment and the atmosphere here encourages drivers, if their approach is correct, to get closer to the team. Some teams don't like that, and treat the drivers very much as contracted employees, end of story. We like to think that we can bring them close to the team."

Nurturing Rubens Barrichello has become a habit in the Formula One paddock. Eddie Jordan was the first, back in 1993. Then Ayrton Senna took him under his wing. After Jordan, 'Rubinho' moved to Jackie Stewart's Ford team, where the Scot went out of his way to make him feel at home, and he responded both in and out of the car. Stewart warned Barrichello not to go to Ferrari, and there may have been times when he wished he had listened, not least when he was ordered to move aside at the Austrian Grand Prix – not once, but twice in successive years.

Time and again, this man with the winning smile has also endured the cruellest failures of the car and the team around him. The worst moment came when he ran out of fuel in Brazil in 2003 when it seemed that, for the first time, he would be able to win in his home town of Sao Paulo.

Even when he has won, a shadow has sometimes been cast over the podium. In Hungary in 2002, Schumacher set the fastest lap of the race by a country mile, but then just sat in Barrichello's wheeltracks. Michael then accidentally handed him the victory at Indianapolis with his infamously botched 'photo finish'. All this has been grist to the mill of Barrichello's detractors, most notably in the Italian media, but still the beatific smile is never far away. The accomplished victories at Silverstone and Suzuka in 2003 were important to 'Rubinho'.

The Brazilian may have fallen short in his task of taking points away from Schumacher's rivals to the same extent that Irvine managed, but then, Schumacher had seldom needed as much assistance since Ferrari hit its stride. He has accepted his fate at Schumacher's hands and proved himself to have the pace, on occasion, to ask some big questions of the master. History will show that this has been as much as anyone could have done... if only he could win in Sao Paulo.

The biggest question confronting Ferrari in the longer term is what happens next. Regime change, when it comes, has the potential to be brutal. The successes of the past eight seasons have all been achieved through dedication to the cause of Michael Schumacher, as much to Scuderia Ferrari. It will be Todt's legacy to ensure that the right people are in place to carry on – sporting and technical directors, design team, and star driver.

The 2003 season revealed just how much Ferrari owed to Michael Schumacher. Those keeping a close eye on Schumacher's in-car camera noticed that he was forced to work harder to get the F2003-GA around the twisting, undulating A1-Ring than they'd seen in years. He was – as he would all year – constantly correcting the car's trajectory and fighting for the ideal line, constantly asked to produce something special – and delivering when it mattered.

On his Austrian qualifying lap, Schumacher was confronted with a thunderous provisional pole position from championship leader Kimi Räikkönen. The Ferrari cut the first sector beam a staggering 0.2 seconds down on the McLaren, before locking up the brakes and arriving in Turn 2 almost completely sideways.

All seemed lost, but Schumacher, unwilling to surrender any further ground, simply applied himself to outright speed on this lap, as he had seldom been called upon to do in recent years. At the end of an eye-watering display he punched the air with glee having beaten the Finn by 0.039s. The F2003-GA had precious little say in the matter.

Sure enough, Schumacher went on to win the race, but the championship lead remained with the youngster Kimi Räikkönen. The decade between Schumacher and the new generation of Räikkönen and Fernando Alonso weighed heavy on the German's shoulders, forcing him to dig deeper inside himself than he had at any time since sealing Ferrari's restoration at Monza in 2000 – and not just in one defining race of the season

In the five races between his inspired victories in Canada and Italy, the depth of Schumacher's slump in form was not, in many minds, entirely attributable to Bridgestone's pummelling at the hands of Michelin, or to any weakness in the Ferrari F2003-GA.

To finish behind Williams was understandable, behind McLaren and Renault acceptable, but Toyota? Jaguar? These were humdrum also-rans... and when was the last time that the world's greatest racing driver finished a lap down on the winner? Unbelievably the answer was at Brazil in 1992.

Having trailed home in eighth place to clinch his record-breaking sixth world championship Michael Schumacher looked gaunt and declared that he felt 'empty'. There was no victory leap, no public celebration in the pit lane. He alone had carried Ferrari through the performance gap to Williams, through the persistent rumours of his impending retirement, through tyre controversy and through the rising tide of young stars eager to usurp him.

At no time before had he looked so much like a man in need of a rest. At Suzuka it was easy to believe that the attractions of a private life with his treasured family, the prospect of losing himself in the wilderness of the Rocky Mountains and dedicating more time to his charitable work might well have appeared preferable to putting himself through another year like 2003.

Perhaps 2004 will be different, but the day is fast approaching when Formula One loses its magic for Michael Schumacher. Until such time as it does there is no doubt that he will continue to race at the very edge of his abilities, pushing himself harder and further than anyone else in the sport and setting more new records.

"It doesn't have the first priority, but it does mean something to me, to have this number on my count," he said. "Actually I'm very delighted about breaking records, but I will be much more delighted sitting one day on my sofa, retired, when I have a cigar and a beer in my hands, and have the time to think about it."

Above: Rubens Barrichello's contribution to Ferrari's dominance as a team cannot be underestimated. Here he celebrates after claiming his second victory of 2003 at the season finale at Suzuka. (Getty Images/Bryn Lennon)

Above right: Felipe Massa starred in 'junior' formulae, and then proved to be as raw as he was fast in Formula One with Sauber in 2002. Many see his later role as a Ferrari test driver as a grooming for stardom, however. (Shell/Getty Images)

Right: Michael Schumacher savours success in his own way, making records that he will appreciate more fully in retirement. (Ferrari)

THE UNFINISHED RIVALRY

"You may not be aware that this is your 41st victory, which puts you in second place, with Ayrton Senna, in the list of all-time winners. Do these records mean a lot to you?" It was this question, during the TV interviews, that triggered Michael Schumacher's tearful breakdown after his victory in the 2000 Italian Grand Prix.

Later, the Scuderia Ferrari Marlboro press release quoted the interview – although Senna's name was conspicuous by its absence. A new explanation appeared instead: "A win after a long winless streak; a win after much criticism in the media; a win in front of the Monza crowd; a win which puts us back in the hunt for the World Championship – and it was a win after two races we thought we had in our pocket and then lost to Häkkinen. It was all too much for me."

Opposite: Ayrton Senna was the only driver Michael Schumacher had a struggle to match, provoking some spectacular racing. (LAT)

There was, however, another argument. The greatest challenge in Michael Schumacher's career was violently lost on that dreadful Sunday in May 1994. No race win, no championship title and no record that he has since emblazoned on the sport has been set against the challenge of a man as consumed with the desire to win as was Ayrton Senna.

For Senna, the threat was evident from the start. "He obviously did a very good job," he said after Schumacher's sensational debut at Spa in 1991. "I don't know much about his background… yet."

It would not take long for intimacy to come. Early in the 1992 season, Schumacher's Benetton trailed the champion's McLaren throughout the Mexican Grand Prix. "It was amazing to follow the World Champion who was my boyhood idol and realise that I was quicker than him while trying to find a way past," Schumacher said, tossing down the gauntlet with wide-eyed insouciance.

A fortnight later came Brazil, where Senna was forced to flex a bit of muscle to keep the pretender behind him while struggling with his gearbox. "He literally prevented me from overtaking him," Schumacher raged. "I don't know what his game was, but it wasn't very pretty. Frankly I don't know why a three-times World Champion has to behave like that."

"He's just a stupid kid," Senna retorted – and the Formula One paddock looked forward to some fireworks.

They arrived in testing for the German Grand Prix when a spate of 'brake testing' sparked a blazing row in the pits, with mechanics scrabbling to free Schumacher from Senna's grasp. "I think he wanted to give me a little massage," the youngster said. "But I don't really think there's a big problem between us."

In 1993 came the lip-smacking prospect of Senna's McLaren and Schumacher's Benetton sharing the Ford V8 engine. Senna saw it rather differently. "We know they have a better engine," he said. "Our engine here is two steps down from Benetton's." The desired inference was clear: 'If he beats me, it's not because he is in any way my equal.'

Through the season, their tallies were: Senna, five wins and one fastest lap; Schumacher, five fastest laps and one win.

When the Brazilian finally got his longed-for seat in a Williams-Renault for 1994, he seemed to feel that the title race was as good as won, especially in view of the new ban on all electronic 'driver-aids'. "I want to be challenged by my own limits and by someone who is born of the same skin and bone, and where the difference is between brain and experience and adaptation to the course," Senna said, delighted at the prospect.

Senna was, however, denied his chance to compete against a youngster now clearly made of similar mettle. The Williams-Renault FW16 was, in its early form, an unruly brute, and the triple champion was powerless to stop Schumacher taking victory in the first two races although, to Senna, the concept of being beaten by the 'stupid kid' was inconceivable.

Arriving at Imola, he was asked how he felt about the 20-point deficit. "Our season starts here," he smiled, refusing to acknowledge Schumacher's existence. Just as he had done with Alain Prost, Senna had abandoned the Queensbury Rules and was preparing for a long psychological battle with the one man who stood between him and the World Championship.

As that horrible weekend unfolded, Senna's emotions frequently threatened to run away with him. He stayed by Barrichello's bedside after his young compatriot's terrifying crash on Friday. On Saturday, he commandeered the Safety Car to see the carnage of Roland Ratzenberger's accident for himself. He took pole position but, although now heavily modified, the Williams remained unstable, and he warned team mate Damon Hill to avoid the bumps on the apex of Tamburello. That night, he rang his girlfriend,

Adriane, in tearful disarray, not wanting to race. After dinner with friends, he called her back: "I'm prepared to sit in the car and step on it," he said.

Six years later, at Monza, Schumacher dried his eyes after the TV interviews and, taking a deep breath, went into the press conference for the written media. Amid an awkward hush, their questions were all easy, underarm lobs about the race – until the very end. "Was your emotional response anything to do with Senna?"

"I think at certain moments not all questions you care to put, or which you would like to be answered, will be answered," Michael said quietly. "I don't like to go into the detail of this question."

Chapter Seven

WITH A LITTLE HELP FROM THEIR FRIENDS

Partnerships forged in motorsport are seldom enduring: they last only as long as they are fruitful. By this measure, the partnerships of Scuderia Ferrari have been well chosen, to say the least. The Swedish based SKF company, for example, has supplied Ferrari with bearings and other components for its drivetrains ever since the first Tipo 125 of 1947. Shell also has a history in partnership with the Scuderia that goes back to its earliest days.

Pre-eminent as the main source of racing fuels and lubricants throughout the 'golden age' of motorsport, Shell saw something more than just another customer in Enzo Ferrari's bold venture. At the start of 1931, Ferrari brought Shell's technicians together with Edoardo Weber to breathe life into the team's ageing Alfa Romeo engines. The carburettor that ultimately evolved – the trumpeted, twin-throated Weber – remains the template for performance induction to this day. It was the first success of many until 1973, when the world fuel crisis forced Shell temporarily out of the sport.

After many successful seasons with McLaren, Shell returned to Maranello in 1996. For Ferrari's engine director, Paolo Martinelli, the relationship is vital, and not simply because, without fuel, his creations would be quite redundant. Martinelli has established strong technical links with the company.

Shell's involvement in Formula One tests Mike Copson and his team to the maximum, but the rewards of being a part of Ferrari's winning team are huge. (Shell/Getty Images)

Left: Together through thick and thin from the outset, Shell's history with Scuderia Ferrari dates back to the early 1930s. (Shell/Getty Images)

Below: Shell's technology gives Ferrari the opportunity to 'see' inside its engine, giving the car a 'blood test' after every run. (Both Shell/Getty Images)

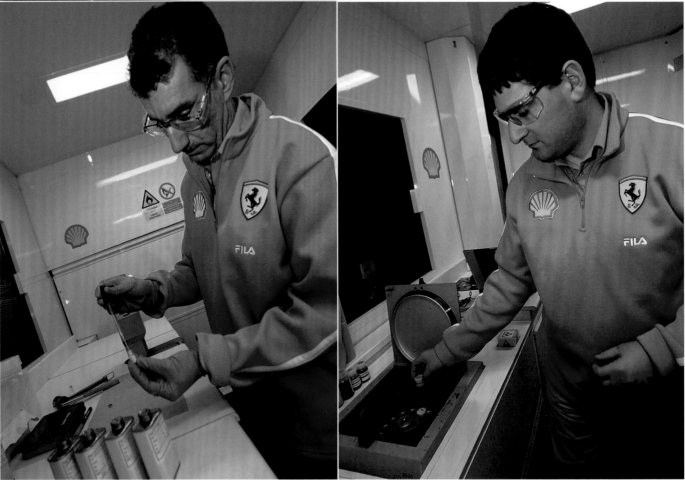

"We are partners," he said. "We have a Shell expert based here for lubricants development, we have continuous meetings, we have joint activities here on the dyno in Maranello to develop the fuels and the oils. We have a common goal so we work together to optimise the engine design with the fuel and lubricant design. For reliability, the optimum lubrication system is one of the most important parts, and the support of Shell in making this part has been very, very important."

The results of Martinelli's drive for reliability have been mightily impressive. Michael Schumacher suffered only two engine failures in 50 races between the start of 2000 and the beginning of 2003. As soon as the word 'Shell' is mentioned in Maranello, or 'Ferrari' mentioned at Shell, it takes about three seconds for 'integration' to spring to someone's lips, but it is not a word lightly bandied about.

What it means to Ferrari is opening up its closest-held technical secrets for scrutiny by the men from Shell and, in Formula One, that is tantamount to marriage. To the Gestione Sportiva, Mike Copson is Shell. If that is a heavy burden, he carries it with ease. Despite a furious schedule and more time spent in the air to attend races, tests, Maranello and Chester than is strictly advisable, his is about the sprightliest figure you will find in Formula One.

"There are 40 people who work on the project and, in the course of the year, we supply 250,000 litres of fuel and 40,000 litres of oil to cover the entire spectrum of factory running, track testing and race support," Copson said. "Formula One is a zero tolerance environment on late delivery, so you can't overestimate the performance of the logistics staff here."

In terms of a modern family car, that is 50 years' supply of petrol being delivered each year to more than 20 destinations around the world. The relationship between what we mortals put into our 'pride and joy' and what Scuderia Ferrari Marlboro uses to win motor races is altogether closer than first impressions might suggest.

It has been FIA policy to ensure that Formula One fuel is as closely related as possible to what gets us down the high street. This is the reason why Shell, together with Mobil, Castrol, TotalFinaElf, Petrobras and Texaco, are engaged in a World Championship of their own. "Ninety-nine per cent of the fuel has to be from commercially available refinery streams, and that means what is available to you and me at the pumps," Copson explained.

"Fortunately, Shell is a global company, so it has the luxury of being able to choose refinery streams from around the world. That, combined with the one per cent of freedom that we have in the rules, means that our blends give a significant benefit to the Ferrari engine.

"A road car will run on the Formula One fuel. It is extremely close to our premium products and, in the past, we have run the car on those products to demonstrate the parallel. The Ferrari fuel is very specifically tailored because a Formula One car never has to start at -30°C, and the fuel never has to have the same cleaning characteristics as a road car fuel. But there is a direct two-way transfer for us, because it's the same guy in the same lab who develops both our road and race fuel."

Constant development of the fuels and lubricants is essential, but careful maintenance of what goes into the engine and transmission is as essential as tending to the hardware itself. Copson and the Shell race team are a fully functioning unit within the Scuderia throughout every Grand Prix weekend.

"We have a full laboratory that travels inside the race truck and it's open throughout every event," he explains. "On flyaways, the same equipment is transported by air in a unit on its own. There's no letup in the level of support we can give in analysis of fuel and lubricants. With the fuel, it's a case of ensuring that it doesn't deviate from the sample held by the FIA."

As well as ensuring that his own team's work is up to scratch, Copson and the rest of Shell's team within Ferrari can also, uniquely, keep tabs on what is going on within the engine and transmission. As a result, the Yeti has been spotted more frequently in recent years than a Ferrari pulling out of a race trailed by a large, blue cloud.

"Our mobile lab has an X-ray spectrometer that can effectively provide a blood test for the engine on-site," Copson continued. "It identifies the amount and types of metal that are in the oil, and provides a wear rate indicator

that allows us to flag up anomalies from our database, and allows the team to take action before a problem develops. It's not common but not unheard of, and it's a unique facility in the paddock."

For Gilles Simon, architect of the Ferrari V10 engines from the outset, this level of intimacy with Shell has been a particularly strong feature of life at Maranello. Simon: "We take the fuel and lubricant as an equal part of the engine development, and Shell has special topics that we need to address, just like crankshafts or camshafts or valve trains. They have a group of dedicated people and these guys are really deeply involved in development. They understand what we are doing and we understand *almost* all what they are doing!"

Copson and the rest of the Shell team put their product inside a Formula One engine – somewhere very few people ever get to see. And the real magic of Formula One, according to Copson, is out of public view. "When, as an engineer, you see the F2003-GA stripped down in the factory, you find yourself looking at the very fuzzy line

between engineering and art," he enthused. "It is incredibly compact, incredibly well thought out. The thing that always amazes me is that these structures produce 300rpm a second. That engine draws in the fuel and air mixture, burns it, and gets it out the other side 300 times a second. *And* it holds itself together."

Another relationship on which Scuderia Ferrari depends is that with Bridgestone, its tyre supplier since 1999. Since 2002, the relationship has gained further momentum because Ferrari's leading rivals, West McLaren Mercedes and BMW.WilliamsF1, have joined forces on Michelin rubber. This has accelerated the symbiosis between Ferrari and Bridgestone.

Hiroshi Yasukawa, Bridgestone's director of motorsports: "We started our Formula One campaign in 1997 and in 1998, given that it was only our second season, we had a brilliant year. I think it was our performance in 1998 that attracted Ferrari's interest in Bridgestone's tyres.

"Goodyear pulled out of Formula One at the end of 1998 and, as of 1999, all the teams were supplied by

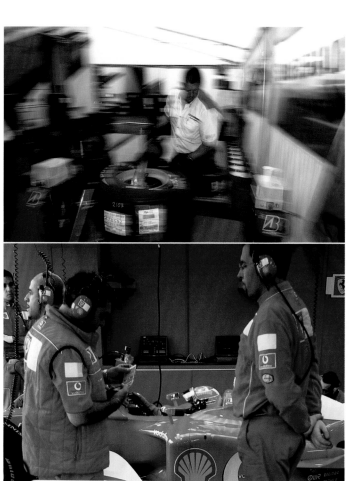

Grand Prix
products for
Ferrari

Bridgestone. It was then that I think Ferrari really understood that they were behind McLaren, who had been using our tyres since 1998 – they had a year's start. And, as a result, Ferrari tried hard to learn how to use our tyres. At the same time, Jean Todt contacted me personally – it was the beginning of a very good relationship."

A very good relationship is one thing, but the demands of Ferrari go beyond the convivial, and deep into the exploration of every possible performance gain. Ross Brawn's all-out style of leadership as its technical director demands nothing less than the maximum from himself and those around him, which is a challenge both Shell and Bridgestone – along with Ferrari's other partners – have met successfully.

Brawn: "There are many areas where it's necessary or desirable to have technical partnerships, to bring enough expertise to the problems and objectives that we have. One is tyres. Another is fuel and oil.

"The tyres are absolutely critical to our success. And, again, it's so competitive that you need a relationship, you need a partnership with a tyre company that is more than just a supplier agreement. You need to analyse data together and you need to share problems and you need to share solutions. The days are long gone of the tyre supplier turning up with a truck full of tyres and saying: 'Try these and see what you think.' That's not the correct approach any more."

This determination – to cement the partnerships, to harmonise the efforts not only of the Gestione Sportiva workforce but also those of Shell and Bridgestone – is as overpowering in the flesh as on the track. Nobody skips a beat in the ongoing dialogue. Words and phrases recur with metronomic precision among all three companies.

Copson explained the rigours of keeping up with life at Maranello: "We react to Ferrari's requirements. It's that

Opposite: There are those who might suggest that there is not much glamour in fuels and lubricants...
(Shell/Getty Images)

Top left: Bridgestone works hard to keep its teams firmly on track, keeping its engineers well drilled to keep up with the workload of Ferrari and the other Bridgestone teams to exacting standards.
(Shell/Getty Images)

Bottom left: Rather than simply sponsoring the team, partners like Shell and Bridgestone sign up to joining in Ferrari's relentless quest for domination – and must put their own reputations on the line along with the team's.
(Shell/Getty Images)

simple. This year [2003], for instance, with the late change in the qualifying procedures, we suddenly had to create a fuel that was as powerful as last year's, but also had a significant increase in fuel economy to give the team the flexibility it requires. And while we react to what Ferrari requires, Ferrari reacts to what we can give them. For example, Gilles Simon might have an idea and we can go to him and say: 'Ah, but we have new technology that can help your combustion enhancement'."

The depth of these relationships can be ascribed to a single factor, according to Ross Brawn. To his eyes, the harmonious view shared by everyone who works within Scuderia Ferrari follows a clear trail through time: "Shell is a company with which we share problems and solutions on both sides. I think that's the way in which Ferrari is different to how it was ten years ago. We have much closer technical relationships with these companies now than were either possible or even wanted ten years ago."

Ten years earlier, of course, was when the architect of Ferrari's success came to power. The mindset Jean Todt

spent so long nurturing gained much from his personal experience of the divisions that confronted him when he arrived. His appointment, his work in bringing the English way of working to Maranello, his decision to install a German superstar in the cockpit – these things broke many previously sacred rules.

Todt: "We are an international team. We know that the German has a different mentality to the Englishman, the Italian, the Frenchman. There is an even bigger difference of mentalities when European people are dealing with Japanese people. So it is just a question of trying to understand, trying to respect each other, trying to take into consideration the motivation of different people coming from different parts of the world.

"Sometimes people in Formula One are very arrogant. But I think that, in the way you lead your life, even if you are very determined and if you have big ambitions, you must be very humble. You must try to make yourself available for others.

"That's what we have tried to do with Bridgestone. We

This wooing of Bridgestone's support, burgeoning into the union of 2002–03, has been a key factor in Ferrari's campaign for Formula One domination. If it took three years of hard work to establish on Ferrari's part, it may have been because Bridgestone had enjoyed a similar strength of partnership with Mercedes-Benz.

"We first worked with AMG Mercedes in 1991," explained Yasukawa. "Mr Domingos Piedade contacted us and we started to work together in the DTM. We dominated. And after that, we moved on to the FIA GT series with Mercedes. A very good relationship developed between Bridgestone and AMG.

"Later, when we entered Formula One, there hadn't been any prior contact with McLaren. Our philosophy was very much one of taking it step-by-step. When we started in 1997, we had confidence we could beat Goodyear, but it was not until Domingos Piedade and Norbert Haug introduced us to McLaren that our relationship with the team began."

Opposite: Ferrari is generous in its praise for its technical partners and, as Bridgestone's Hiroshi Yasukawa joins in the 2002 championship celebrations, he can reflect on a job well done. (Shell/Getty Images)

The outcome of this relationship was the spectacular success of McLaren-Mercedes in the first half of 1998, and the dramatic response of Ferrari in completely rethinking its F300 chassis. Ultimately Ferrari lost that battle but, as Bridgestone took over the exclusive Formula One tyre supply in 1999, the Scuderia embarked on a race to match McLaren's experience of the tyres.

Left: Ferrari's partners are prepared to stretch every sinew to carry Michael Schumacher to championship success. (Shell/Getty Images)

The 2000 season was a difficult balancing act for Bridgestone, with the Ferraris initially far, far harder on their rubber than the McLarens. Meanwhile, away from the overall title battle, the third contender, BMW.WilliamsF1, spent the 2000 season helping Michelin to get up to speed for its return to the fray. A dedicated BMW-Williams-Michelin team pounded round the test tracks all year before the declaration of a new 'tyre war' in 2001.

The arrival of Michelin ensured that the need to win over Bridgestone's intimate support became crucial to both

have tried to respect them, to listen to them, to give them space and credit, and to make them trust us and listen to what we were saying. Slowly, slowly, we've built something that's unbelievably strong."

For the Bridgestone brand, success in Formula One has meant giant strides in the European passenger car tyre market. But the day-to-day life for the Bridgestone Motorsport Formula One team in Langley, England, is focused on the strength of its bond with the Gestione Sportiva.

Hiroshi Yasukawa: "In this business, one of the major issues is trust. If you have trust, then you can do good business. The people at Ferrari tried hard to understand the Japanese mentality. Not only Jean Todt and Michael Schumacher, but throughout Ferrari, everyone tried to understand our way of working and even our way of living. With the support of Mr Montezemolo, our relationship strengthened even further. Ferrari's attitude was very different. Now we are not just a supplier. If there is a problem, then we help each other."

Ferrari and McLaren, which added another element to their on-track rivalry. Williams, alone as a potential race-winner on Michelin's books, could be very specific when it came to its tyre demands. But 'compromise' is a word absent from the vocabularies of both Ross Brawn and Ron Dennis.

It came as both a surprise and a relief, therefore, when McLaren made a dramatic switch to Michelin before the 2002 season. Its decision cannot have been easy.

Yasukawa: "Our relationship with McLaren remained excellent in 2001. They undertook some extremely important testing programmes for Bridgestone. We gained a lot of information, good data, from those tests, which was passed on to our Technical Centre in Japan. Unfortunately, towards the end of 2001, to our surprise and disappointment, McLaren informed us that they would switch to Michelin."

Ross Brawn: "There's no doubt that one of the things that contributed to our success in 2002 was the decision by McLaren to go with Michelin. It cleared the way for us to have a very clearly and tightly focused partnership with Bridgestone, without the distraction of another serious competitor bringing alternative information, challenging different directions we wanted to go in, compromising Bridgestone's line of thought.

"It was very obvious that Bridgestone were going to give Ferrari priority in the design, development and choice of tyres. Strategically, McLaren moving away from Bridgestone was one of the best things that could have happened for us."

If this news was welcomed by Ferrari, it also meant redoubling the effort if every last ounce of an advantage was to be wrung from the new relationship. Bridgestone was still also supplying Sauber, Jordan, BAR and Arrows but, to keep ahead of Michelin (and retain that boom in European sales), what needed to be done was clear to Yasukawa: "Jean Todt understood exactly what was needed

and he immediately authorised a special team to work closely with us. So now Ferrari had a specific tyre test team, which was very important. What was also important was that Ferrari had a good, fast and reliable car. This was crucial if our tyre tests were to be beneficial. The cooperation we received from Ferrari was huge."

And, as it transpired, *vice versa*. Ferrari was delighted with the results of the strengthened partnership. The F2002 redefined Formula One design, using all the expertise of the Gestione Sportiva to produce the tiny gearbox and all the other refinements that brought the most dominant Formula One performance witnessed by a generation. As the high-flying F2002's only contact with planet Earth, the tyres were central to that performance, and Bridgestone's technical input crucial.

Race team manager Luca Baldisserri explained: "During practice, it's difficult to predict what the tyres will do in the race. Often you can't do a stint of 20 laps – you can do a stint of eight laps maximum. But you have to try to understand from those eight laps what the tyres will do on Sunday. So Bridgestone's engineers help us to analyse the tyres – checking the temperatures, checking the blisters. They help us to forecast the tyre behaviour in the race and to make the correct choice between the compounds."

Throughout Ferrari's long road to union with Bridgestone, Shell was already defining the standard of the partnership expected by Jean Todt and Ross Brawn. Although not as visually clear as the relationship between the chassis and the track surface, the fuel and lubricants have undergone an equally extensive programme of refinement to produce championship-winning results.

Mike Copson: "Once we have established what's required, we go through a process. We use computer simulation and trial blends to create a matrix of fuels or 'lubes' that the team can try, according to what it wants to address in the characteristics of the engine. It might be more performance, better economy, improved wear protection. We can tailor fuel to various circuits if required.

"In 2003, for instance, the logistics that were required for the first three races, being so far away, meant that we only had one type of fuel available at the tracks. And it was a new blend at the start of the year. We improved it, and then we had a totally new fuel ready when the new car appeared in Spain. This isn't about supplying a standard fuel."

Partnership with Scuderia Ferrari is clearly one of the most demanding processes on which Shell, Bridgestone and the team's other technical suppliers could embark. However, there is no trace of resentment over the supreme effort that is constantly required and expected by the Gestione Sportiva, for two reasons.

First, there is the desire for perfection that comes with exposure to such a high level of competition. Shell and Bridgestone have seen the results on the track in victory after victory. But these companies are keenly aware that they are up against the best in the world and, as the uneven start to the 2003 season exposed, the threat of losing that hard-earned domination is ever present.

Second, there is the spirit of unity engendered by Jean Todt. This hardest of task-masters takes care to nurture its technical partnerships, to show a softer side. In July 2003, the long contribution of SKF Automotive was acknowledged with a 'Ferrari Innovation Award' at the third annual Podium Ferrari ceremony in Maranello. SKF was honoured for its "Continuous ability to innovate, supplying bearings of the highest possible standard for the Formula One single-seater and the Ferrari and Maserati Grand Turismo road cars." The award was personally presented to SKF Automotive vice-president Riccardo Dell'Anna by Ross Brawn, Paolo Martinelli, Michael Schumacher and Rubens Barrichello.

For the men put on the front line by the team's technical partners, just being intimately involved can be reward enough, as Mike Copson enthusiastically observed: "The amount of technology, the standard of design and the thoroughness of application that goes into making those two cars run through a Grand Prix weekend never ceases to amaze me. As an engineer, it's impossible to run out of things to be staggered by – in the design, the materials, the technology, the electronics. It's simply awesome. It's an honour and a pleasure for us all to be a part of it."

TEAM WITHIN A TEAM

Out of sight for almost the entire year, there is a constant, detailed drive for perfection by Scuderia Ferrari and its partners, enacted by a 60-strong group of engineers who turn the inventions of the design team into race-winning reality.

The test team is led by 'Gigi' Mazzola, another of the career-long Ferrari men, who arrived at Maranello in the mid-1980s to work in the calculation office before graduating to design, and later joined the race team for 1990 as Alain Prost's race engineer.

Since 1995, his role has been to ensure that every single component of the package is tested to destruction, analysed in full, and then tested again by the most advanced research and development team anywhere in the motor industry.

Secret warriors: Luigi Mazzola's test team puts in enormous effort to ensure that nothing is left to chance in the design and operation of Ferrari's Formula One cars. (Ferrari)

For Jean Todt, the concept of such a satellite operation is a necessity, rather than a luxury. "It's like wind blowing," he said. "You must make sure that you're always going in the right direction. You need to have people very focused on medium- and long-term programmes as well as on daily programmes to make sure you don't lose direction."

The work rate by Ferrari's test team is nothing short of phenomenal. In 2002, for example, lead test driver Luca Badoer logged 120 days pounding round Ferrari's private test track at Fiorano and the Ferrari-owned Mugello circuit in Italy, and in Spain on the Circuit de Catalunya near Barcelona, at Valencia, at Jerez. "Badoer does an incredible job for the team, and he's fast, too," enthused Rory Byrne. "He's consistent and he's very fit. He can do four, five days no problem at all, at 400km a day. He takes it in his stride."

Badoer was joined in 2002 by former Jaguar Racing driver Luciano Burti, who worked on the Bridgestone programme, and in 2003 by Felipe Massa.

The table overleaf shows the schedule for developing the outgoing F2002 and the incoming F2003-GA as it was fitted in around the first flyaway Grands Prix of 2003.

Ferrari Testing February–March 2003

DATE/WEATHER	CIRCUIT		DRIVER (CHASSIS, JOB)	LAPS	BEST
03/02/03 6–16°C – sunny	Barcelona Length: 2.937m	Record: 1m20.355s	Schumacher (F2002, tyres) Barrichello (F2002 tyres)	88 64	1m17.282s 1m16.900s
04/02/03 12–16°C – dry	Barcelona Length: 2.937m	Record: 1m20.355s	Schumacher (F2002, tyres) Barrichello (F2002, tyres)	85 65	1m15.465s 1m15.762s
05/02/03 3–14°C – sunny	Barcelona Length: 2.937m	Record: 1m20.355s	Schumacher (F2002, electronics) Barrichello (F2002, tyres)	105 54	1m15.103s 1m15.408s
11/02/03 1–6°C – sunny	Fiorano Length: 1.849m	Record: 57.476s	Schumacher (F2003-GA, shakedown)	78	57.045s
11/02/03 7–19°C – sunny	Valencia Length: 2.48m	Record: 1m10.143s	Barrichello (F2002, electronics)	116	1m10.963s
12/02/03 1–6°C – sunny	Fiorano Length: 1.849m	Record: 57.045s	Schumacher (F2003-GA, shakedown)	8	56.807s
13/02/03 1–3°C – cloudy/snow	Fiorano Length: 1.849m	Record: 56.807s	Schumacher (F2003-GA, development)	84	56.786s
17/02/03 3–6°C – cloudy	Imola Length: 3.063m	Record: 1m24.170s	Schumacher (F2002, tyres) Schumacher (F2003-GA, development) Badoer (F2002, set-up)	8 43 15	1m24.250s 1m21.617s 1m25.090s
18/02/03 0–8°C – sunny	Imola Length: 3.063m	Record: 1m24.170s	Schumacher (F2002, set-up) Schumacher (F2003-GA, development) Barrichello (F2002, simulation) Badoer (F2002, set-up)	23 34 26 15	1m21.795s 1m21.980s 1m22.739s 1m23.022s
19/02/03 3–8°C – sunny	Imola Length: 3.063m	Record: 1m24.170s	Schumacher (F2003-GA, development) Schumacher (F2002, tyres) Barrichello (F2002, simulation, tyres)	42 52 68	1m21.532s 1m20.441s 1m21.541s
21/02/03 4–19°C – sunny	Fiorano Length: 1.849m	Record: 56.786s	Massa (F2002, systems, set-up)	86	57.751s
25/02/03 9–10°C – wet/dry	Jerez Length: 2.752m	Record: 1m23.135s	Schumacher (F2003-GA, electronics) Schumacher (F2002, tyres) Badoer (F2002, tyres)	20 31 1	1m25.321s 1m26.447s N/A
25/02/03 6–19°C – sunny	Fiorano Length: 1.849m	Record: 56.786s	Massa (F2002, electronics)	37	57.954s
26/02/03 10–17°C – sunny	Jerez Length: 2.752m	Record: 1m23.135s	Schumacher (F2003-GA, development) Schumacher (F2002, shakedown)	53 1	1m25.626s N/A
26/02/03 20°C – sunny	Fiorano Length: 1.849m	Record: 56.786s	Massa (F2002 race chassis, shakedowns)	16	57.581s
27/02/03 11–17°C – sunny	Jerez Length: 2.752m	Record: 1m23.135s	Badoer (F2003-GA, development) Badoer (F2002, simulation)	26 89	1m20.041s 1m19.573s

DATE/WEATHER	CIRCUIT			DRIVER (CHASSIS, JOB)	LAPS	BEST
27/02/03 3–9°C – sunny	Fiorano Length: 1.849m		Record: 56.786s	Massa (F2002, electronics)	70	57.378s
28/02/03 18°C – sunny	Jerez Length: 2.752m		Record: 1m23.135s	Badoer (F2003-GA, development) Badoer (F2002, electronics)	39 8	1m18.954s 1m19.920s
28/02/03 8–13°C – cloudy	Fiorano Length: 1.849m		Record: 56.786s	Massa (F2002, electronics)	39	57.780s
11/03/03 12°C – cloudy	Mugello Length: 3.259m		Record:	Badoer (F2003-GA, development)	4	Accident
12/03/03 15–21°C – sunny	Fiorano Length: 1.849m		Record: 56.786s	Massa (F2002, tyres)	143	57.782s
13/03/03 6–12°C – sunny	Fiorano Length: 1.849m		Record: 56.786s	Massa (F2002, tyres)	122	57.496s
14/03/03 8–13°C – sunny (track watered)	Fiorano Length: 1.849m		Record: 56.786s	Massa (F2002 tyres)	160	57.066s
15/03/03 8–10°C – cloudy	Fiorano Length: 1.849m		Record: 56.786s	Massa (F2002 tyres)	16	57.920s
25/03/03 10–24°C – sunny	Barcelona Length: 2.937m		Record: 1m20.355s	Barrichello (F2002, tyres) Badoer (F2003-GA, development)	75 57	1m17.750s 1m18.822s
26/03/03 10–18°C – sunny	Barcelona Length: 2.937m		Record: 1m20.355s	Barrichello (F2002, tyres) Badoer (F2003-GA, development) Badoer (F2002, tyres)	87 35 30	1m17.964s 1m17.571s 1m18.465s
27/03/03 12–20°C – bright/cloudy	Barcelona Length: 2.937m		Record: 1m20.355s	Schumacher (F2002, tyres) Barrichello (F2003-GA, simulation)	98 85	1m17.794s 1m17.335s
28/03/03 13–17°C – cloudy/wet	Barcelona Length: 2.937 m		Record: 1m20.355s	Schumacher (F2002, tyres)	40	1m19.044s
29/03/03 12–18°C – sunny	Fiorano Length: 1.849m		Record: 56.786s	Schumacher (F2003-GA, development) Badoer (F2002, electronics)	90 20	56.338s 58.818s

Chapter Eight

AT THE RACES

It was Sir Frank Williams who made the point that Formula One is a business 24 hours a day, seven days a week – except for a couple of hours every other Sunday. The technical development, the wheeling and dealing, the corporate commitments, the fearsome politics and everything else are stilled just long enough for a Grand Prix to happen.

Since 1999, the strength in depth of the Ferrari organisation as a whole has been emphatically proven. All the commercial deals, all the men and women who work in the Gestione Sportiva, all the days of testing, all the computer power, wind tunnel work and brainstorming sessions are focused on the moments between the lights going out and the fall of the chequered flag.

'Twas ever thus, of course. All these endeavours, all this energy and thought process and programming is designed towards something that has remained virtually unchanged since 1906, beneath the surfeit of glitz and gloss that has been applied in the modern era. It has been a case of refinement, first and foremost to the Formula One Technical Regulations that govern the cars, but also to the circuits themselves and the races that they stage.

What actually constitutes a Grand Prix has been a moveable feast since the inception of the phrase in 1906. Races have been staged over a pre-set number of laps, a pre-set mileage and/or a pre-set duration of anything up to two days (in 1906) or a solid stint of 10 hours (in 1931 – long before 'The Show' became a consideration). In the modern era, the world's Grands Prix have been steadily harmonised

With tens of thousands of pieces of information to unravel every lap, everyone at the circuit is kept busy deciphering every element of the team's performance. (Shell/Getty Images)

since 1981 when Bernie Ecclestone took charge of their promotion and, more important, their TV exposure. To enable live broadcasts to be scheduled, races have been run over 190 miles or two hours, whichever comes sooner (with the exception of Monaco, where 160 miles is the target distance given good weather).

In 1991 came the election of Max Mosley to the presidency of the world motorsport governing body, the Féderation Internationale de l'Automobile. Mosley had long been seen as Keith Richards to Ecclestone's Mick Jagger, and the format of the Grands Prix was further refined after his election. Mosley's motivation was driver safety, first and foremost, and his vision was to bring the average lap speed under control, preventing it from creeping above 130mph – widely agreed to be the jumping-off point between speed and safety. First came curbs to the technology then developing in the form of electronic 'driver-aids' and sophisticated hydraulic suspensions, alongside which Safety Cars were introduced – and, for 'The Show', mandatory refuelling stops.

Before this first raft of changes could truly be assessed came Imola 1994. With two drivers dead and one injured, together with several bystanders, draconian measures were put in place with immediate effect. The imposition of extra chicanes on the circuits, and vents in the airboxes of the cars to sap power, reduced speeds substantially. With the reduction in engine swept volume to 3-litres, the adoption of grooved tyres and other adjustments, Mosley appeared to have prevailed.

Throughout these years of transition, the circuits became far more harmonised under the influence of Hermann Tilke, the FIA's approved circuit designer. Through Tilke's labours, Imola was transformed almost beyond recognition. The bite was taken out of Spa's celebrated Eau Rouge big-dipper without losing its visual impact, the infield course at Indianapolis was created, the Nürburgring adapted, the first chicane at Monza reprofiled, high-grip asphalt laid instead of gravel at Silverstone, the epic sweeps of Hockenheim and the rolling speed of the Österreichring condensed into a more modern format.

Add to this the crowning glory of Sepang in Malaysia and the projected circuits in Bahrain and Shanghai – not to mention Istanbul and maybe Bangalore – and it is clear that Tilke has been extremely busy. He has had a strict template within which to work: one that enhances driver and spectator safety at every opportunity, and keeps the average lap speed down to 130mph.

Into these homogenous amphitheatres came the Scuderia Ferrari Marlboro team at full strength, intent on domination and also with clear operational parameters. From Kuala Lumpur to Northamptonshire, there is as much uniformity as possible. This has played into the hands of Ferrari in its seasons of domination.

No matter where Formula One travels in the world, the routine is the same. The cars and equipment arrive either in trucks or, at the 'flyaway' races, in crates, on the Tuesday. Through the Wednesday, the pits and paddock are prepared so that on, on the Thursday, the trucks – having been precisely parked-up to the organiser's satisfaction – are emptied and polished while the racing cars go through the scrutineering process. The pit garages are laid out ready for action, the motorhomes and kitchens are readied, the fridges and espresso machines plugged in, the tables laid.

Like any other team, Ferrari must look after its team members, technical partners, sponsors, media visitors and VIP guests alike. To this end, it has two motorhomes at each of the European rounds (Ferrari's own for VIPs and Marlboro's for the team, the media and other guests), providing a flavour of home for all who enter their air-conditioned splendour.

At the 'flyaway' rounds, the hospitality vehicles stay home, but the caterers continue their labours undaunted in America, Australia, Brazil, Canada, Malaysia and Japan, transforming each air-conditioned suite into a home from home. This means, on average, preparing 1200 meals each weekend – and, with media *soirées* and home events, the total reaches well over 200,000 over the full season. It is indeed fortunate that the Italian staple of pasta is largely unaffected by the vagaries of climate, and ready to eat in minutes.

As all the catering and hospitality preparations are made, the team prepares the garages in pit-lane. Floors are laid, hoardings erected, tool cabinets fitted. The pit boxes are marked out, and most important of all, the telemetry equipment is rigged up on the pit wall, in the back of the garage and in the data truck.

Data-acquisition in Formula One, pioneered in the early 1980s, has reached a point where 150,000 readings per second are taken of the engine, transmission, suspension, steering and tyre systems while the car is on the move. In all, the 17 races generate around 40 gigabytes of information, all harnessed to the mission of going faster for longer than anyone else.

Ferrari has put this information to use within the philosophy of Jean Todt's leadership: never trying unproven components, never forcing the pace of development, painstakingly harvesting and processing information. All through its years of superiority, the results have been clear right from the start of every race weekend, the free practice on the Friday morning.

Other teams often play themselves in gently, but the Ferraris have consistently been at or

Opposite: Every Grand Prix is the culmination of months (even years) of preparation, working night and day to turn invaluable data into on-track performance. (Ferrari)

Above: In order to increase efficiency, the race team is now housed in its own dedicated logistics centre, where the exact requirements for every race are rigorously evaluated. (Ferrari)

above the previous year's race-winning pace within the opening minutes. Senior engineer Luca Baldisserri: "There's no gamble on Fridays at all. The baseline set-up is usually based on the previous year's conditions, from the history of our car at that particular track. It's based on the list of the problems that we could have – particular corners, particular bumps, stuff like that. Wind direction is important for any particular track. Also we have results from a computer simulation model that we constantly develop through the year here in Maranello. Typically we have a good confidence that, from the beginning, it is very close to the optimum."

For most drivers, this situation would be a great luxury. Michael Schumacher likes to use it to demoralise his opposition. Nowhere more so, perhaps, than at the challenging road course of Spa-Francorchamps, the ultimate driver's circuit, which is seldom used during the course of each year and can consequently pose set-up problems.

The usually moist air of the Ardennes forest can make for some lurid sights as the cars first go out onto this track, but watching the number 1 Ferrari rocket downhill into the double-left of Pouhon on a Friday morning is a sobering experience. Where others feather the throttle, noses shimmying around for grip as the camber falls away from them, the Ferrari fairly shrieks in, its

Above: For the honoured few VIPs and media invited to Ferrari's inner sanctum, there is a warm welcome to be found in the paddock hospitality units. (Ferrari)

Opposite: Michael Schumacher at speed. While the rest of us can only look on in wonder, the Scuderia has come to expect nothing else. (Shell/Getty Images)

champion driver banging down the gears and braking later than many would attempt in qualifying. Instantly he jumps back on the throttle with his mount clinging to the hillside, apparently defying all the laws of nature.

That is why Ferrari has always been prepared to pay handsomely for Schumacher's services. His commitment is immediate and unwavering, his lap-times as unerring a guide to the team's engineers as their telemetry readouts.

Until 2003, the Friday was traditionally a day of fettling, of setting-up the cars during two free practice sessions, both in full race trim with their fuel cells half to three-quarters full, and stripped-down in qualifying trim, with enough fuel for one screamer of a lap. Sometimes a midfield runner with sponsors to impress would put out a car with every tweak in the book (and a few more besides), thus to set a blistering lap-time and grab a few Saturday morning headlines. In the pits, meanwhile, the more methodical engineers would pore diligently over the cars and the computer screens and the printed readouts, looking for the optimum compromise of tyre wear, wing angles and suspension settings, switching gear ratios, fussing over engines.

All that was abandoned at the end of 2002 as 'The Show' took over once again. Ferrari having won 15 races in that season, public apathy confronted the sport. It seems that domination at Ferrari's level simply could not be tolerated: something had to be done to retain the TV appeal of Formula One.

Abruptly Friday was designated in the Sporting Regulations as the first of two qualifying days. And each day's session was reduced to a 'one-shot showdown' as each driver drove a single flying lap with the circuit all to himself. The device had long been used with promotional success in IndyCar racing, and had also been adopted for Touring Cars and World Superbikes.

The Friday morning was also 'reinvented' as a two-hour test session for those teams agreeing to forego more than 20 days of private testing (and thus to save the expense of booking circuits). The FIA decreed that the other teams must make do with minimal running time on the track on which they were about to qualify and race. The expectation was that the teams with relatively small operating budgets –

the target group for Friday testing – would be able to put those two hours to good set-up use, and get themselves further up the grid order.

Unfortunately these new Sporting Regulations did not quite live up to that expectation. As U2's Bono once sang, the rich stay healthy and the sick stay poor. The gap between the very front of the grid and the very back increased by half a second. The FIA was relieved that it had introduced another new Sporting Regulation, awarding championship points to the first eight finishers, instead of only six – occasionally, in the past, only the cars entered by the three wealthiest teams.

Nonetheless there remain millions of expectant viewers, listeners and readers around the world wanting to know what's going on, and at least the FIA made plenty more time available for the PR side of Formula One.

Each day of a Grand Prix weekend includes trips by the driving stars of every team to the Paddock Club, where the high achievers and honoured customers of the sponsors assemble to be pampered with food, drink and all-round VIP treatment. A little light banter with a Master of Ceremonies might precede a description of what it is like to drive the circuit, a few thoughts on the race to come – and then smartly away, leaving the salesman of the month and his small child equally agog.

Back in the paddock, there is more of the same. The days of journalists collaring team members and getting candid comments are long gone, replaced by gatherings in the motorhomes most evenings, and the daily FIA press conferences in the media centre.

Condensing opportunities for journalists down to a few half-hour bursts means that tempers can often be frayed. Mind-games and paddock politics are played out before a silently baying mob. Questions that are either infuriatingly open-ended or bitingly honed must be fielded. The results can often be spectacular, usually when Michael Schumacher is around.

There is inexhaustible interest in Ferrari's champion, particularly in his contentious ways, such as his habit of chopping off rivals when they are going to the first corner. "Can you tell me whether the situation today, where complex rules of engagement dictate what drivers can and can't do to defend a position, is better than that in operation in the 1970s?" came one question. "Namely that drivers would race fair and square, instinctively knowing what was 'on' and what wasn't?"

"But," Michael countered, bristling, "the press situation has changed in the last 20 years too."

"Yes… it's much harder for us to get access to you lot these days." Amusement everywhere but in Schumacher's direction.

"This is not the point," he said.

"I agree," his tormentor pressed on, hackles raised. "So why did you raise this red herring, and why don't we get back to the question I asked you initially?"

Such battles of wit are a regular feature of the Grand Prix media experience. It is easy to forget that English is not the mother tongue of Schumacher or Ferrari. Yet the German in particular has perfected clear defences, battering troublesome questions into submission with standard phrases such as: 'Honestly I'm telling you' (*ie* 'Call me a liar at your peril'). And: 'If you look' (*ie* 'I can prove I'm right – can you?').

Dealing with meddlesome media is not an issue for Luca Baldisserri and the Scuderia's other engineers. "It's a very light fight between the team, the engineers, the drivers and the press people or the marketing people," he said. "I don't remember a situation where one of the drivers came back distracted because of a bad interview or a bad press conference. At the beginning of the weekend, we get a media and marketing schedule, so we know when the drivers or Ross or the engineers will be there and when they won't.

"Maybe sometimes it's hard, but basically we might look at a job and realise that we have to do it in five minutes, because we know that in five minutes someone has to go and give an interview. The communications department has got better at this every year. It's not a problem for us."

Amid all the trackside activity surrounding the cars and the world that watches them, their creators are seldom seen. Everything is out of their hands by the time the cars arrive

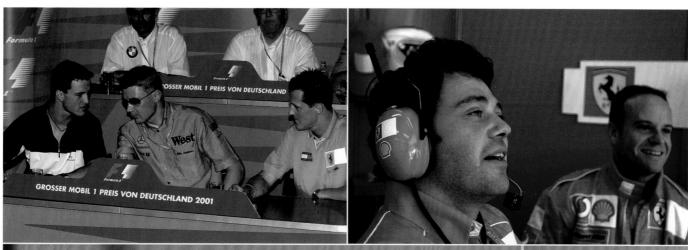

at the circuit although, every so often, they do appear, wraith-like, to keep an eye on things.

"The actual race I watch with my wife and son on the TV," said Rory Byrne. "There might be a panic at the track in a certain area but, generally, everything is so specialised nowadays that if there's a problem with, say, the hydraulics system, then really I wouldn't be able to help with the detailed knowledge that's required. The head of our onboard systems would be called in, because he has much more specific knowledge of that particular area of the car."

Byrne chooses to enjoy his races, going only to the two Italian events each year to get a sniff of the atmosphere and catch up with old friends. Gilles Simon is a slightly more regular presence, but enjoying the races is far from the bearded Frenchman's mind.

"I can't be really relaxed when there's a car running," he said. "Especially in a race, when anything can happen. There is always a big question mark: have we tested properly? Are we sure about everything? It's difficult not to be slightly nervous."

How reassuring, then, is the presence of Ross Brawn on the pit wall. This is the man styled as Ferrari's master tactician, the creator of the Scuderia's endlessly varying strategies on fuel stops, tyre choices and all the settings on the cars. "The race is the icing on the cake," he beamed. "If the ingredients and the baking are no good, then we're

wasting our time. The important thing is all the essential work that's involved in getting to the icing. But I've always enjoyed working through the strategies. It's something I wouldn't want to delegate because it's the final step."

Although delegation might not always appeal to Brawn, he is surrounded by strength in depth when it comes to planning the weekend's strategies. On hand are the fuel and lubricants experts from Shell, the tyre technicians from Bridgestone, and his own engineers, who have been led for season after season by Luca Baldisserri.

"I personally developed the strategy software, and Ross is using it very successfully!" Baldisserri said with well-won pride. "We start work on the strategy the week before each race when we sit together around a table to discuss the steps we want to take. So before we get to the circuit, we have an idea of the strategy already. We tune this idea during the race weekend, reacting to the tyre behaviour through the practice sessions, what the car is doing, how the fuel and lubricants are performing.

"So it's basically a job of fine-tuning our ideas through the weekend and, hopefully, we finally come up with something better on Saturday night. We have three or four possible plans on Saturday night and then, after the warm-up on Sunday morning, we know which plan we are going to take. This is not the end, though. Several times in a typical season, we have to change our plan during the races.

We have to check what our competitors are doing, and look at all the different options to make the correct responses."

With united and skilful technical, test and race teams optimising chassis and engines that have increasingly been the class of the grid, for the world's best driver, it is small wonder that Scuderia Ferrari Marlboro has been able to win championship after championship. Even so, the results of Jean Todt's 'dream team' are astonishing.

To some they are little short of infuriating – rivals and some quarters of the media most of all. Good fortune has played its part – although Schumacher has claimed the lion's share of luck next to his team-mates – and sheer circumstance has led to endless conspiracy theories.

Perhaps the most famous example was Schumacher's 1998 British Grand Prix win, which he took whilst trundling through the pits to take a 10-second penalty for overtaking under yellow flags. He was allowed to keep the win because of considerable delay on the race officials' part in asking him to stop, much to the displeasure of McLaren's Ron Dennis, as it cost his man Mika Häkkinen his fourth win of the season and made a title race out of an apparent McLaren whitewash.

Judged against the supreme Williams-Renault, the Ferrari F310 was uncompetitive in 1996, but Schumacher won three times. The following year's F310B was compromised but, even so, the title was within reach until the last 30 minutes of the season. In 1998, McLaren-Mercedes started off with half a season's advantage over the rest of the field but only won at the final round, thanks to the massive development programme lavished on the F300.

In the period 1999–2002, Ferrari only built on the domination that it fought so hard to achieve. Its 2002 campaign was as close to perfect as any in Formula One history – as McLaren well knows. Of Ferrari's 15 victories, no fewer than 11 fell to Schumacher, another new record. It could easily have been bettered if he had chosen not to sit behind his team mate in Hungary or Italy, or indeed if he had not forgotten where the finishing line was at Indianapolis while staging *that* 'photo finish'.

The 2002 Drivers title was also in Schumacher's pocket in record-breaking fashion: only 140 days elapsed between his victory in Australia in March and his title celebrations in France in July. Schumacher's form never even looked like dipping. He completed every one of the 17 races and, more to the point, he finished on the podium without exception. His was the biggest winning points margin ever seen – 67 points clear of Barrichello.

Watching on at home in Maranello, as Enzo Ferrari had once done, the architect of the F2002 delighted in every lap. Rory Byrne: "It's just great to win, isn't it? I mean, the thing that impresses me most, and gives me most pleasure, is the consistency with which we've run at the front. We ran over 50 races without being off the podium. It's that sort of consistency of performance at the top that gives me the most satisfaction."

It is also the sort of consistency that draws fire. As success begat success for Maranello, the rest of the paddock grew restless. With the onset of a global economic slowdown, the other teams were suffering. Prost Grand Prix and Arrows Grand Prix International went to the wall – the latter having scored fewer points in 23 seasons than Ferrari achieved in 2001 alone.

So it was that the FIA tore up the rulebook for 2003. The Formula One show looked pale next to the thrills and spills on offer in 2002 from the football World Cup, and the Ryder Cup golf. Trackside crowds fell and visible gaps appeared in the grandstands. More important, the TV figures plunged 23% through the course of the season as the MTV generation passed sentence. The days when viewers were enthralled merely by sporting genius have been consigned to history with the clicks of millions of TV remotes.

"Formula One can be hard to explain, because it's a fact that it's complicated," sighed Ferrari PR man Luca Colajanni. "Football is the most popular sport in the world because it's the easiest to understand. You have one pitch, 22 players on two sides, two goals... It's never different. Formula One is different because so much of what happens is done by people you don't see. OK, we have 17 people at a pitstop, six people on the pit wall, and TV viewers do see some of them. But the people inside the garage analysing the

Opposite, left: Attention to detail brings Ferrari victory after victory, and tyre maintenance is high on the agenda. (Ferrari)

Opposite, right: Jean Todt is a master of paddock politics, which are as much a part of the race weekend as what happens out on track. (Shell/Getty Images)

data, the people working back at the factory – you can't show all of them."

Like everyone at Scuderia Ferrari Marlboro, Colajanni is clearly highly motivated by his sense of being part of such a magnificent team effort: "You can't show how our people read the telemetry, how their interpretations influence the race strategy, how the people from Shell and from Bridgestone contribute to the strategies. It is something that we will remember forever."

For many TV viewers, on the other hand, the racing in 2002 was instantly forgettable. As it became obvious that no one could match the scarlet cars through 2002, FIA president Max Mosley and Formula One Management promoter Bernie Ecclestone appeared to espouse some truly insane ideas for spicing up 'The Show' – adding 'success ballast', forcing the drivers to swap cars on rotation and so forth – in the hope, surely, that these would take the sting out of whatever changes were to come.

The teams – outraged by these schemes – were invited to put forward ideas themselves. It is built into the structure of Formula One that they require unanimity to implement changes. In these and any other circumstances, this was as likely as walking to the moon. The team principals would never be able to agree on what time of day it is.

They can argue that black is white, and white is black, like no one else, and with more conviction. Their discussions went in circles and back to nowhere.

Finally, Mosley delivered the body blow, just weeks before the start of the 2003 season. Rather than impose new rules, he said, he would simply reinterpret existing rules in a new way, and make changes to the Sporting Regulations. There would be no recourse for the teams, because the FIA has full command over all such rules. Only the Technical Regulations cannot be changed at short notice without the agreement of the teams.

A package of new Sporting Regulations was put in place with immediate effect, headed by the introduction of single-lap qualifying over two days. Clearly this kind of qualifying process would tempt the top teams to produce special cars for the two sessions, built to run only on an out-lap, a very quick flying lap, and an in-lap. The FIA had thought of that. An addendum stipulated that, immediately after Saturday qualifying, all the cars were to be taken from the teams to *parc fermé*, where they would be held until released the next day to form the starting grid. Any attempt to refuel them, alter their settings or change their tyres was prohibited (unless for clear safety reasons).

So it was that, when Formula One returned in 2003, it was superficially the same but infinitely different in the detail. To many, it seemed as though the new rules were aimed squarely at the pillars on which Scuderia Ferrari Marlboro had built its domination, and that all the other teams were being invited to take a good, long run-up and finish the job of kicking them down. Little details, such as Friday qualifying being run in the order of the current Drivers' points table (so that the leading drivers would run when the track was at its dirtiest), gave the game away.

Yet Ferrari met the new rules with surprising equanimity. Jean Todt: "One must consider that the entire world was going through its worst economic crisis since 1929. The only certain thing was that a reduction in costs was in the best interests of everyone. Clearly one team might be in favour of a modification but not another, with another team adopting a third view. Somehow there had to be a situation that suited all the parties involved."

In fact, of all the teams, it was Williams and McLaren which objected most vociferously to the new regulations. They jointly embarked on a public war of words with Max Mosley. In an open letter to the FIA president, Sir Frank Williams and Ron Dennis accused him of 'dumbing down' Formula One.

Mosley responded in kind, accusing the Englishmen of being 'unfocused'. He said: "If you truly believe that the public want to see computer-controlled cars, guided from the pits by anonymous engineers, please think again. If you don't believe me, hire two halls in any city anywhere in the world and put, for example, Michael Schumacher, Kimi Räikkönen and Juan-Pablo Montoya in one, with both of you plus your electronics experts and your technical chiefs in the other. Invite the public to either hall and see what happens."

Malaysia was another poor show – Barrichello third and Schumacher sixth after a first corner tangle with Jarno Trulli's Renault – and Brazil was a disaster. Amid a downpour, Schumacher aquaplaned off the circuit to end his run of 24 points-scoring finishes, although when the rain clouds lifted it was Barrichello who was poised to win his home Grand Prix at the eleventh attempt when his car coughed and died. 'Fuel feed problems' said the team – a bitter joke, for there simply hadn't been any fuel left in the tank.

Missing from the pit wall at these opening races of the new era was Luca Baldisserri, who had felt he had achieved about as much as he could for the team, and had asked for a transfer. "I have to say that winning both championships, after ten years of working at it, was a good situation," he said. "After winning both titles three times, I asked Ferrari for a new situation, for new challenges. For sure it had been fantastic, so good I have no words to describe it. But as an engineer you want to achieve the top and, when you achieve that, you want something different. For a driver, it's different. A driver always wants to win, he wants to break records. Engineering means you need different challenges. You can't stay in the same thing for a long time."

Despite taking one pole position, leading two of the first three races and setting two fastest laps, and in the previous year's car, Schumacher became a target as the capricious Italian media went berserk. By one partisan reporter, the defending World Champion was labelled 'a baboon'. Rumours of Ferrari's demise were premature, however.

Ross Brawn had said the previous Christmas: "I know that at some stage we're going to level off. We're going to have a period where we lose races and perhaps lose the championship. But I think we're strong enough to see that as a new challenge and get back to where we want to be." It had been a prophetic statement.

Baldisserri was swiftly restored to the race team. Back in Europe from the 'flyaways' and at home for the San Marino Grand Prix, Scuderia Ferrari rallied as it had not needed to since 1998. Still driving the F2002, Schumacher gave the most successful car in Ferrari's history a memorable send-off, taking pole position, then duelling with his younger brother Ralf's Williams-BMW before taking off into the distance.

The British teams duly fell silent, and the new look 2003 season got underway in Melbourne – albeit with a familiar pair of red cars filing the front row of the grid. The F2002s took off into the distance, leaving an entertaining race behind them as the fast racers made their way through the fast qualifiers on a wet-dry circuit, but for the first time since September 2000 a day of racing ended without Michael Schumacher heading the World Championship table.

The performance was all the more remarkable because, in between qualifying and the race, he and Ralf had hurried back to Germany to say farewell to their mother, Elisabeth, who had fallen badly at home. She had passed away overnight.

Imola 2003 stands as one of Schumacher's finest drives because, emotionally, it was the most difficult of them all.

Straight away the eagerly awaited Ferrari F2003-GA was pressed into service, and Schumacher soaked up the altogether more welcome pressure of Fernando Alonso's burgeoning superstardom to take his second successive victory. He won again in Austria despite a momentary blaze while refuelling, but in Monaco the Williams-BMW team took flight, and Schumacher, four points behind Kimi Räikkönen, faced an uphill struggle.

The Canadian Grand Prix should have been a whitewash for Williams, but an inspired Schumacher stole the race from under them, pitting his guile with relish against the sheer pace of the Michelin-shod teams, and sneaking into the championship lead. It was a day of celebration that would have to sustain him through a long, hard summer.

Raring to go: the 2003 Scuderia Ferrari Marlboro Formula One team pose proudly with the F2003-GAs after a victorious debut in Spain. (Shell/Getty Images)

On its home track at the Nürburgring, Mercedes pulled out all the stops for Kimi Räikkönen and McLaren. However, what should have been a crushing victory literally disappeared in a cloud of smoke, and to Stuttgart's shame the BMW-powered Williamses scored a jubilant 1-2, while the number one Ferrari languished in fifth place.

A second clean sweep for Williams followed in France, but then came Silverstone, and Rubens Barrichello's day of days, thanks in no small part to the intervention of a deranged and defrocked Irish priest playing chicken with the cars. In spite of this, Rubens put in a mighty performance. Diving past car after car into the Abbey chicane, and overtaking Räikkönen through the daunting Bridge bend, he took the most popular victory of the year bar none – although for Ferrari the worst was yet to come.

In Germany, Barrichello's race only got as far as the first corner. Fortunately for the team the accident in which he found himself included Kimi Räikkönen and Ralf Schumacher – the latter subsequently relieved of $50,000 for being held responsible for an avoidable accident. Michelin tyres meanwhile kept the top six finishers in touch with the asphalt, led by the Williams of Juan Pablo Montoya and followed at a respectful distance by the seventh-placed Ferrari of Michael Schumacher.

Hungary saw the youngest ever podium in Formula One history… and Michael Schumacher wasn't there. Fernando Alonso put the nimble Renault to use on the sultry twists of Budapest, this time leading a seven-car sweep for Michelin. Schumacher was again the top Bridgestone runner and this time he was eighth, claiming the desultory point that was intended for the likes of Jaguar or Minardi rather than a title contender.

Three weeks of intensive testing later came the Gran Premio d'Italia at Monza.

In the Ferrari pits nobody even spoke, lest the absolute concentration be broken. After toughing it out side-by-side with Juan Pablo Montoya for half a lap, Schumacher converted his pole position into euphoric victory – his 50th for Ferrari and the fastest race in Formula One history – with his low downforce Ferrari streaking past the delirious tifosi at 233mph.

Crisis? What crisis? Monza reinvigorated Schumacher and Ferrari's title challenge, but Indianapolis was an abject lesson in fortune favouring the brilliant. Juan Pablo Montoya should have won by a mile but instead blew a fuse, crashing into Barrichello as the rain fell to leave Schumacher, Ferrari and the wet-weather Bridgestones to take the win and almost, almost the championship.

Mathematically, Kimi Räikkönen – with one win to Schumacher's six – had a chance of bringing the Ferrari era to a premature halt, courtesy of some serious reliability. At the season finale at Suzuka, he would have to win and Schumacher would have to fail to score a point – an unlikely scenario at the start of the weekend, but fate would push the young Finn tantalisingly close to glory. Qualifying fourteenth to Räikkönen's eighth, as the race got underway Schumacher moved slowly up through the field, crashed into a BAR, pitted for a new nose, and went straight to the back, while his title rival made his way into second place.

Out in the lead was Rubens Barrichello's Ferrari, but you wouldn't give tuppence for the Brazilian's luck, and Schumacher certainly couldn't stake a sixth world championship on it, painfully working his way up to claim the final point that would put the title beyond Räikkönen's grasp.

It was a scrappy day's work, brother Ralf bearing the brunt of the action, suffering a big old chop as he pulled alongside the Ferrari on the pits straight, and then getting his nose knocked off under braking for the chicane. For once, Rubinho's luck held, with Räikkönen powerless to get on terms with another great drive from the Brazilian.

It may as well have taken place on another planet though, for all eyes were on the somewhat distant form of the number one F2003-GA.

Sure enough Michael Schumacher laid Juan Manuel Fangio's 46-year-old record of five titles to rest, and both the drivers' and constructors' championships were rescued from the brink. Despite the fact that during the 2003 season Ferrari had won more races than Williams, McLaren and Renault put together, it had taken some monumental performances by both Schumacher and Barrichello to stave off regulatory upheaval, advancing rivals, personal tragedy and media frenzy, for eight long months.

Small wonder that it was a somewhat bewildered Schumacher who stared fixedly out at the world in the aftermath. "It hasn't really sunk in yet, I am empty and exhausted but proud of what we as a team have achieved with another constructors' championship," he said. "If you see what has happened at Hockenheim, in Budapest, how many people wrote us off, how many people wrote things about us, outspoken things. And here we are, we're back."

Later on the champion recovered his senses somewhat, making up with brother Ralf over a few celebratory drinks. With the pressure off at last, the two brothers wrought havoc through the evening – wrecking the Toyota hospitality area with the assistance of Olivier Panis.

The sight of their champion wearing the remnants of a Toyota uniform whilst indulging in rock'n'roll excess might have caused a few of the residents of Maranello to choke on their breakfasts the next morning. Yet there were few who would begrudge him a release from the phenomenal pressure of the previous season – and many who would chuckle 'bravo, campione,' glad to see that there was life in the old dog yet.

PUBLIC IMAGE LTD

"I don't think it made any difference to the spectators, to be honest. It was a great race and it didn't make any difference."

As Ross Brawn uttered these immortal words in the pit-lane at the A1-Ring at the end of the 2002 Austrian Grand Prix, he had to shout to be heard. The noise was not coming from the track. It was coming from the grandstands.

For the second year in succession, they had arrived in Zeltweg with Michael Schumacher enjoying a massive lead in the championship. For the second year in succession, Rubens Barrichello had got the better of his team leader. And, for the second year in succession, Barrichello had been asked – and finally ordered – to move aside for his partner.

Schumacher had indulged in ill-advised waving on the slowdown lap, punching the air in jubilation. This was quickly abandoned once his helmet was off and he could hear the noise. The crowd was pointing and waving and screaming at him… but for all the wrong reasons, and to the accompaniment of pencils being sharpened in the Media centre.

Scuderia Ferrari has never had an easy time of it in the media – whether it has been losing or winning. Formula One is a global sport, stirring strong emotions from Sao Paulo to St Petersburg – and Ferrari is by far its most evocative name. This sobering fact has never been lost on Jean Todt.

Enzo Ferrari would sit at home and read about the comings and goings of his team in the newspapers before deciding what actions to take, if any. Ferrari may have gone, but Italy's partisan press still savours its role as the team's

judge, jury and executioner – and it calls for Todt's head with astounding regularity.

"Something which would be pretty natural to any other team always takes big propulsion here, because people need to write stories about Ferrari," said Todt, with visible displeasure. "Unfortunately they don't give us as much peace as we need – unlike our competitors."

With the eyes of the world upon them, and newspapers keen to sell copies, life in the Scuderia's press office, headed by Luca Colajanni, is seldom dull.

"Michael did his first test of 2003 and he spun on the first lap," Colajanni laughed. "He just very, very lightly kissed the barrier. Immediately a website correspondent in Barcelona wrote a note on his site, then Reuters made a news item about it, then the German press took it and did the same, then the Italian press called, screaming: 'Whoa! Michael had an accident!'

"I haven't seen anything, ever, about a McLaren or a Jordan when it spun. Whenever I talk to a journalist about stories like this I ask: 'Do you really have to do a story because Michael spun? OK, you can do it, but do you do the same for everybody?'

"But this is just a measure of the importance of Ferrari."

Nowhere, of course, is Ferrari more important than in Italy, where Formula One ranks alongside football as the national sporting preoccupation.

Colajanni: "A section in the Italian daily newspapers and the Italian TV news is set aside for Formula One. In our newspapers, it's at least half a page about motor racing every single day. Of that, 90% will be about Ferrari. This space has to be filled. Often I get calls from colleagues saying: 'Help me please! What can I write?'"

In recent seasons, the Italian media have had wonderful success to report and, to some extent, their teeth have been drawn. But success is not the only reason. It is a hallmark of the Todt era at Ferrari, particularly since the arrival of Michael Schumacher, that no unwarranted (nor even warranted) accusation can precipitate the downfall of the team. Instead, it is met either with a complete rebuttal or with silence – if necessary, irrespective of the evidence at hand.

Ferrari's pursuit of World Championship success has not always been kind to Rubens Barrichello, who had to move aside for Schumacher in two successive Austrian Grands Prix. (LAT)

Chapter Nine

THE
RIVALS

Since the emergence of Vanwall in the mid-1950s, the most prolific winners in Formula One – except in the dominant years of Scuderia Ferrari – have all hailed from Britain. Cooper, BRM, Lotus, Brabham, Tyrrell, McLaren, Williams and Benetton were all products of a thriving cottage industry of small, specialist firms that sprang up in the days after World War 2.

Throughout the first half-century of motorsport, Britain eschewed the motor racing fever that swept mainland Europe and the USA. Horse racing was the 'sport of kings', cricket and rugby were the favoured sporting pursuits for the gentry, football was the working class opiate. The idea of nationalistic clashes of technical mastery found little favour, even when Selwyn Edge drove a Napier to victory in the Gordon Bennett race of 1902 and, in 1907, Brooklands became the world's first permanent race track.

Britain's Society of Motor Manufacturers & Traders actively campaigned against the sport. Even as the great automobile makers of the world built their 'grandee' teams, the SMMT banned racing cars from its annual Motor Show for being 'vulgar and irrelevant'. The British viewed this sport merely as an idle pursuit for wealthy enthusiasts. Only the bloody-mindedness of men like W.O.Bentley, Sir Malcolm Campbell, Raymond Mays and Earl Howe did anything to reverse the situation when they formed around them the British Racing Drivers Club.

After the war, however, came the revolution. There was an attempt by Mays, a co-founder of ERA which had built

Three of the best: Michael Schumacher is coming under increasing pressure from the likes of Kimi Räikkönen (right) and Juan Pablo Montoya – the three rivals finished 1-2-3 in the 2003 Drivers' Championship.. (Shell/Getty Images)

'voiturettes' for rich customers in the 1930s, to fill the void left by the 'Silver Arrows' of Germany and establish BRM as Britain's national team, but at first it was a dismal failure. The baton was passed to Vanwall, a team founded by millionaire businessman Tony Vandervell to showcase his advanced bearings, brake discs and 'thin wall' engines, which won the inaugural World Championship of Constructors in 1958 before running out of steam.

Now the specialist engineers took over, pitting thrift and invention against the relative grandeur of European-style racing, with John Cooper and Colin Chapman leading the way. The plethora of redundant military airfields scattered over England, now being used as makeshift race tracks, offered smooth surfaces relative to the European road circuits, and encouraged the evolution of radical, lightweight, highly adjustable racing cars. It was Cooper who placed the engine behind the driver – a layout pioneered by Benz and Auto Union between the world wars. In the late 1950s, the little single-seaters of Cooper and Colin Chapman's Lotus, although powered by the humble Coventry-Climax fire pump motor, began to outperform the front-engined Ferraris, race-bred on uneven European roads.

Opposite: BMW.WilliamsF1 has fought hard to mount a consistent challenge to Ferrari's crown with the skills of Ralf Schumacher (left) and Montoya. (LAT)

Cooper and Lotus paved the way for Brabham, McLaren, Tyrrell, Williams, Surtees, Hesketh and many more – all powered by the Ford Motor Company. In 1966, inspired by the vision of Walter Hayes, Ford committed itself to building an affordable, race-winning Formula One engine (and Team Lotus introduced corporate sponsorship to pay for it). Subsequently its benchmark Cosworth DFV swelled the grids with ambitious new teams of varying pedigree.

In Maranello, Enzo Ferrari often despaired at the temerity and pace of the DFV powered 'garagistes' but, through the 1970s, the old order was gradually restored, with his Scuderia again on top. Then Lotus took racing technology into entirely new areas, and Brabham, McLaren and Williams also began to set new standards. A whole new way of life was created, ideas zipping from team to team as engineers were drawn to the thriving Formula One scene.

Among them was a fresh graduate by the name of Ross Brawn, who arrived at Williams in the mid-1970s.

"It wasn't an intended career path," he said. "I was very keen on engineering, and I saw this job being advertised, so I went along on the off-chance to see what it was all about. I didn't really care if I didn't get the job. In fact, I was the second choice, but the guy who was offered the job thought it was all a bit risky, and turned it down. Whoever he is, I owe him a beer!

"That was back in 1976, and I worked for Frank for a year as a technician and machinist. The teams were very small in those days so we all did a bit of everything. Frank then actually lost his team: he was in some financial difficulty and he had to sell out to Walter Wolf. I left for a year to work on a Formula Three team, but then Frank reinvented himself and I rejoined. That was really the beginning of Williams Grand Prix Engineering, and the lead up to the two World Championships which we won while I was there."

A glowing affection for this era of Formula One is evident in all who were there. Williams and his partner Patrick Head focused their little team around the unlikely figure of Alan Jones, a burly Australian charger who shared the all-or-nothing mindset of the Englishmen, as much as their hitherto unpromising form. "Three lads out there together, having lots of fun," was how Head put it.

Brawn: "I think I was very fortunate in that I joined motor racing when the teams were very small. It was fun. It's regrettable that we can't really give people the same sort of experience that Rory [Byrne] and I were able to get. Formula One was so small back in the late 1970s, and even in the 1980s.

"When I joined Frank the second time, there were 11 people there, so I had to machine parts, I had to fit them to the car, I had to drive the truck, I had to fit tyres... We all just did everything necessary to enable the team to progress. I learned an awful lot very quickly. That was a very important period of experience and learning, and then really it grew from there."

Over the two decades before Brawn helped Ferrari back to the top of Formula One, all other competition gradually melted away from the red-hot pace of McLaren and Williams. After taking over McLaren in 1980, Ron Dennis reinvented it as an international marketing showcase, in order to draw in the funds required to introduce advanced composite chassis materials and electronic control systems.

These systems developed beyond recognition through the mid-1980s, thanks largely to Patrick Head at Williams, but McLaren fought back by forging not only a long-term partnership with Honda, but also signing the two best drivers of the era in Alain Prost and Ayrton Senna. Williams responded with the design skills of Adrian Newey and the power of Renault. Meanwhile Ross Brawn, after a period out of Formula One designing Tom Walkinshaw's Jaguar sports-prototypes, was starting to carve a name for himself with the Benetton team.

Once they had Michael Schumacher on board, Benetton began to make inroads into the Williams advantage, until Schumacher was crowned as the World Champion for the first time in 1994. It was the start of an often rancorous rivalry between Brawn and the two 'British establishment' teams, which have questioned the legality of Brawn's Formula One cars on more than one occasion.

"The nature of Formula One is that there is a lot of fuss about whatever's happening," Brawn sighed. "It's part and parcel of the business. But it does hurt a bit, there's no point in denying it. It's just unfortunate that one or two people – and it's no more than that – try to explain their inadequacies by insinuating that someone else is getting an advantage unfairly."

There was a brief cessation of hostilities at the end of 1995, while Michael Schumacher got to grips with life at Ferrari, Tom Walkinshaw transferred to Ligier, and Brawn and Rory Byrne remained with Flavio Briatore at Benetton. When the two engineers returned to Schumacher's side at Maranello for 1997, however, the war of words became thunderous.

The allegations have been many and varied to the effect that rules may have interpreted far beyond their original intent. Flexible wings and floors (banned as moveable aerodynamic aids) were suggested. Aerodynamic 'bargeboards' were found to be incorrectly located. 'Fiddle-

brakes' acting as a form of traction control were discovered – although not on the Ferrari – and the traction control debate generally recycled endlessly (until the FIA allowed it again).

Brawn is familiar with all the allegations and allowed himself a wry smile at their mention: "I don't want to call it an illness, because it's not that serious, but there is a genuine lack of capacity for some people to accept the success of others. I can honestly say I can sleep at night knowing that, if McLaren beat us – and they have many times, and Williams – I would never go into the office the next day and say: 'Those bastards are cheating, it's unfair, they ought to be kicked out.' I come into the office and say: 'Look, guys, they're doing a better job than us – what are we going to do about it? How are we going to redress the balance?'

"I know for a fact that people have said that Ferrari has only beaten them because we're doing something we shouldn't be doing. In a funny way, that helps us. It takes their focus off what's really important. They're not concentrating on how they're going to redress the balance, and get back to winning, because there's 'something going

on'. Michael's driving standards, traction control, team tactics – they use whatever they want as their own means of convincing themselves that our success is not justified or fair."

Within the Ferrari team, there is a favourite *bête noir* at the heart of the paddock – the man whose team has come closest to thwarting Ferrari's dominant years. Rory Byrne: "Ron Dennis is entitled to his opinions, I guess, but really I think our performances have vindicated us."

The genial South African engineer has learned to keep out of the line of fire, but even he can get a touch waspish in return: "The FIA has complete access to our data and to the car, they can check and measure what they like. And they do. They make checks on everything, and we've always had a clean bill of health. I don't know why they say these things: you'll have to ask Ron Dennis. It's definitely water off a duck's back here. I don't even give it the time of day. I hear about it but I don't even read it."

The FIA was unhappy about all the innuendo and matters reached crisis point at the end of 2000. Schumacher and Ferrari had finally brought a level of domination unknown to the Scuderia since the days of Niki Lauda, but the trouble was that the allegations were so vociferous, and the arguments so involved, that the value of the championship itself was being called into question.

Exploiting and explaining the legal minutiae – the letter of the rules *versus* the spirit of the rules – was engaging for those involved, but the governing body knew that the public was becoming disenchanted with the endless bickering. The FIA abruptly announced that traction control would be allowed once again, as from the fifth race of 2001.

For Brawn, the fact that the performance gap remained unchanged is a vindication of Ferrari's arguments over the years of debate: "But they never retracted their statements. It's rather an unpleasant side of the business, but it's just the way that some people are. They can't cope with being beaten. Probably they truly believe that we're doing things we shouldn't, but I just have to accept it."

Just like his technical team, Michael Schumacher has been handed as many brickbats as champagne bottles on the road to pre-eminence. His time at Ferrari has generated numerous rivalries, but none quite so consuming as that with Jacques Villeneuve in 1997.

Villeneuve's Williams-Renault FW19 should have been a bullet-proof title winner but, early in the season, both team and driver managed to shoot themselves squarely in the foot often enough to allow Schumacher to get himself back in the game. The Canadian, who had got himself into trouble with the FIA after attacking its responses to the Ayrton Senna fatality as an 'over-reaction', started the year with a gigantic car advantage over the rest, but Williams promptly started work on its 1998 car. With one or two race strategy hiccoughs, this distraction allowed Ferrari to pounce.

Schumacher's cause was greatly assisted by the deployment of Eddie Irvine as a kind of malevolent court jester, running rings round Villeneuve verbally and winding him up on the track, while Schumacher clawed himself into the lead of the title race until that last infamous round at Jerez. Villeneuve ended the year as the champion but immediately headed for life in the midfield, first with a depleted Williams team in 1998, then with cash-rich newcomer British American Racing.

Schumacher was confronted by an altogether different rivalry with Mika Häkkinen.

It took almost seven full seasons after his quiet, assured debut at Team Lotus in 1991, but Häkkinen had been born to the role. Plucked from the wreckage of the once-great Lotus team by Ron Dennis, who was looking for an eventual replacement for Senna, Häkkinen had to sit out most of 1993 as American IndyCar star Michael Andretti seldom turned down the opportunity for an accident, and Senna made Dennis pay through the nose on a race-by-race deal.

The young Finn earned the undying admiration of Dennis, for sticking with the team when lesser men might have walked. When he sensationally outqualified Senna on his first outing at the Portuguese Grand Prix, the relationship was cemented. There followed a disastrous 1994 with Peugeot engines, before McLaren linked up with Nigel Mansell and Mercedes-Benz in 1995. Häkkinen drove the living daylights out of the brutish MP4-10 but, at the last race meeting in Adelaide, a rear tyre deflated during practice, pitching him into a near-fatal accident.

Remarkably, he survived – not only the accident, but also the winter of recuperation, the lurid photographs and the mental anguish that followed. Again Dennis was impressed by the commitment of his man against adversity. When McLaren Mercedes hit winning form, in 1997, it was David Coulthard who brought home the first victory – but there was seldom much doubt where loyalty lay.

So it was that, in 1998, armed with Bridgestone's full attention and Adrian Newey's MP4-13, Häkkinen destroyed everyone at the start of the season – even his British team mate after their 'pre-race agreement' had handed the Finn the Australian Grand Prix. It is a tribute to Ferrari and Schumacher that they were able to put up any resistance at all, let alone to take the championship to the last round at Suzuka.

As they left the dummy grid side-by-side to start the deciding Japanese Grand Prix, pole man Schumacher – resplendent in a chrome crash helmet and with 100,000 '1998 World Champion' caps readied for sale – stalled his engine. Häkkinen took his eighth victory of the year and his first title. Those surplus red caps burned.

The following year, Newey was less cautious with the MP4-14, producing a lighter, faster, but edgier and less reliable car. It was a golden opportunity for Schumacher, but he was forced out by his Silverstone crash, and Häkkinen prevailed.

In 2000, Ferrari's tub-thumping opening salvo brought three wins in a row which appeared to deflate Häkkinen. This left Coulthard as the effective team leader, despite the trauma of a dreadful air crash, but Ron Dennis went to work on Häkkinen, to produce a blistering run back into contention through the Austrian, German and Hungarian Grands Prix. At Spa he hunted Schumacher down as the Ferrari again beat the life from its tyres, only for Schumacher to chop him at 200mph on the long run out to Les Combes.

Häkkinen responded with one of the most memorable overtaking manoeuvres of modern times, using Ricardo Zonta's lapped BAR as cover to dive inside Schumacher at exactly the same spot. He went on to win the race.

Asked at the press conference if he had been put off by the chop, Häkkinen said: "I knew that, if I got level with Michael under braking again, he wouldn't give me room…" He turned towards the German. "Correct?" The media centre erupted and Schumacher sat chastened. "So I decided to go to Plan B," Häkkinen concluded.

It was to be one of his last shows of defiance. In 2001, Häkkinen was preoccupied, again found wanting in terms of competitiveness. He still managed to win races – at Silverstone and Indianapolis – but he had become a father, he had twice won the greatest prize he could imagine and, frankly, he had seen enough of Formula One.

"Only we two were up there and there was nobody else to follow us," Schumacher reflected after his nemesis had retired. "He was the best man I have been fighting, losing to him or winning against him." As is so often Michael's intention, his praise of Häkkinen also served to undermine his team mate, David Coulthard.

Arriving with a privateer Formula Ford team that put the works entries to shame, Coulthard had been championed by Jackie Stewart, who selected his fellow Scotsman at the start of his campaign to build a 'staircase of talent' to Formula One. It didn't quite go to plan, however. Coulthard lost the 1990 Opel Euroseries title to Mika Häkkinen, and then the 1991 British Formula Three championship to Rubens Barrichello.

By 1993, Coulthard's career seemed to have hit a wall. But then Alain Prost, newly installed at Williams-Renault, paired himself with the team's test driver, Damon Hill, rather than undergo the trauma of teaming up with Ayrton Senna again.

Coulthard stepped up to the empty testing role. Senna got his chance to join Williams the following year but, after

Imola, the Scot had the difficult job of filling the empty seat, which he did with aplomb even after being regularly elbowed out of the way by Nigel Mansell.

Becoming a full-time Williams driver in 1995, Coulthard managed, in the course of the season, both to take his first victory and to drive his car into the pit wall. Ferrari put in a bid for his services as number 2 to Schumacher, but Coulthard elected to pair up with Häkkinen at McLaren instead. Although the Scot brought home the first victory for Mercedes-Benz in 42 years, however, overall he failed to assert himself within the team.

Meanwhile the once cordial relationship between Coulthard and Schumacher soured considerably. The team tactics and psychological warfare that had almost unglued Villeneuve at Williams had little effect on Häkkinen, but plenty on Coulthard. The nadir was reached at the rain-soaked 1998 Belgian Grand Prix when Schumacher rammed Coulthard while attempting to pass him, then hunted him down in the pits and attempted a brawl. "Are you trying to f***ing kill me?" he shrieked.

In 2000, Coulthard won the British Grand Prix and was then fortunate to emerge unscathed from an airplane crash at Lyon-Satolas airport which killed both the pilots. With this new lease of life, he attacked Schumacher as never before, winning the Monaco Grand Prix and then, memorably, taking time out to indicate that Schumacher indulged in onanism while passing him to win the French Grand Prix.

If Ferrari was untouchable in 2001, it was on another planet in 2002, by which time Coulthard had other problems in the form of his new Finnish team mate, 24-year-old Kimi Räikkönen.

When Räikkönen had made his Formula One debut in Australia in 2001, at the wheel of a Ferrari powered Sauber, many objections were raised. He had driven only four races in British Formula Ford and one full season in British Formula Renault (after considerable success in karting), but he had been plucked from the ranks by Sauber's talent spotter, Jacky Eeckelaert. He arrived to a chorus of protestation that he couldn't be up to the job.

Räikkönen barely noticed the fuss. In fact, he almost didn't make the race in Melbourne because of this laid-back demeanour. He fell asleep, as is his wont, while relaxing on the beach, and burned his legs raw. It made his debut drive to sixth place all the more remarkable, and launched him into the Formula One stratosphere.

He was the ideal driver for Ron Dennis – astonishingly fast, not big on talking. "If you want to win – get a Finn," the outgoing Mika Häkkinen had urged his mentor, even if the team itself was a trifle daunted by Räikkönen's mouse-like presence. When asked about Coulthard's seniority, he responded with a quiet: "I don't give a shit." And went on to outqualify the Scot 10 times.

Räikkönen's greatest disappointment was not winning the 2002 French Grand Prix, which he led superbly until hitting a patch of oil at the hairpin with five laps to go, and running wide. It was testament enough to the Finn that Schumacher opted to chop him viciously on the exit of the corner: clearly he felt that a marker was needed for the young pup, even on the day on which he claimed the fifth World Championship of his career.

But for a stop-go penalty for speeding in the pit-lane, Räikkönen would have won the first race of 2003 in Melbourne. As it was he took third place and the opportunity to give Schumacher a dose of the treatment meted out at Magny-Cours the previous summer, sending the Ferrari bounding over the kerbs as he swept imperiously past.

Coulthard won that opening skirmish – somewhat fortuitously after Ferrari, Räikkönen and the Williams of Juan Pablo Montoya all tripped over themselves – and became the first man other than Michael Schumacher to lead the world championship since Monza 2000. The McLaren team appeared a little disappointed though, and when Ron Dennis was moved to tears at the next race in Malaysia, where Räikkönen took the flag, the writing was on the wall for the Scot.

As Coulthard's title challenge went to pot, Räikkönen put in a season-long campaign of pressure from behind,

Opposite, top:
Coming through!
Kimi Räikkönen is
one of the brightest
stars of the new
Formula One new
generation, and
took the World
Championship fight
to the wire in 2003.
(Sutton)

Opposite, bottom:
Oh, brother! Ralf
Schumacher
remains keen to
stamp his authority
over elder brother
Michael at the
wheel of the mighty
Williams-BMW.
(Shell/Getty Images)

logging eight further podium finishes to keep himself in with a mathematical chance of becoming World Champion until the very last lap of the season. All this, despite four times being forced to start either at the back of the grid or from the pits after spinning away his single qualifying lap, defined in sharp relief the Finn's qualities as a racer.

All season he did his level best to keep a car whose foundations were laid two seasons earlier in contention, the only time that he failed to do so being at the Nürburgring when the Mercedes engine let go. He led the championship race from Malaysia in March through to Canada in June and ended the year just three points shy of Schumacher, though he never let himself get excited about it. At 23 years of age Räikkönen knows that there will be plenty of other opportunities in years to come.

As Ferrari continued to dominate Formula One, and McLaren led the fight back, the barren years at WilliamsF1 also melted away, thanks to the power of its BMW engine. The renaissance had begun in 1997 when Bernd Pischetsrieder, then the head of BMW, had persuaded the board to approve a plan to tackle Formula One to win back some of the headlines from the Schumacher/Mercedes title race.

BMW felt its way in gently, opting (unlike Mercedes) to build its own engines rather than to pay for a specialist firm to do the job, and to put its engineers through a steep learning curve by contesting Le Mans with the Williams-built BMW V12 LMP sports-prototype. Victory eluded the new partnership in 1998 when overheating problems were created by BMW's insistence that the race engine should be cooled through little nostril intakes in the nose, just like those on its road cars. In 1999, the engineers held sway over the brand marketing men, and BMW waltzed to victory.

Meanwhile the engine department in Munich put the finishing touches to its V10 Formula One engine. At the first race of 2000, BMW's blue-and-white colours returned to Formula One for the first time since the glory days of Nelson Piquet and Brabham. Not only that, but a Williams-BMW FW22 came home third, driven by a man called Schumacher.

Ralf Schumacher, Michael's younger brother, is an enigmatic character. Having missed out on one of the boys from Kerpen, Mercedes gave Ralf his break with a test for McLaren in 1996 as he added the All-Nippon Formula 3000 title to his Macau Formula Three win of 1995. The team was not impressed, however. In 1997, the younger Schumacher started his Grand Prix career at the wheel of a Jordan-Peugeot.

His debut season was packed with incident – not least taking out his own team mate, Giancarlo Fisichella, in Argentina. There were some mighty accidents along the way, including one at the Nürburging, where he managed to trip up over brother Michael's championship challenge in a kamikaze start that put a serious rent in the family fabric. The relationship with Jordan lasted another year but, after Ralf had been forced to cede victory at Spa to Damon Hill's limping sister car, he moved on to Williams.

It proved to be an inspired move. The 1999 season was something of a boot camp for the brattish Ralf, Sir Frank Williams ready to suffer none of his previous outbursts, but heaping praise on him when it was due – which was often. A podium in the Australian opener was one of eight points-scoring finishes with a car that was poor even in the estimation of its creators.

Come 2000, and BMW was delighted to have the polished Ralf on side. Yet, as the season progressed, he was made to look increasingly ordinary by the sprightly English 'rookie' Jenson Button, veteran of just one season of Formula Ford and another season of Formula Three, who was in turn keeping the second Williams seat warm for the much-hyped arrival of Juan Pablo Montoya in 2001.

Nonetheless it was Ralf who won the team's first race for four years, at Imola in 2001, and he did so in fine style, toughing it out on the grass going into the first corner as brother Michael attempted to block him, and snatching a lead he was never to lose. It was a great performance – and he repeated it with victory at Malaysia in 2002.

At Monaco the 2003 Williams-BMW package came good, courtesy of new Michelin tyres at the front and some revised suspension geometry at the back. Ralf seized upon the FW25's new pace to take an immaculate pole, but on raceday it all went wrong. The sister car of Montoya hounded him to the pit stops and then got past, with the younger Schumacher seeming to lose interest there and then.

After the Canadian Grand Prix there was heavy censure for Ralf's apparent unwillingness to try passing his older brother for the win, just as there had been at the Nürburgring in 2001 and Interlagos in 2002. However, Ralf bounced back to dominate two Grands Prix in a week at the back-to-back European and French races. His dominance, though, only served to reinforce the belief that, while fine when out on his own, Ralf had little of the pure racer in him, and was unwilling to get involved in the rough stuff when required.

What Williams thrives on like no other team is racing, preferring to see a car come back to the pits with its nose missing, rather than pristine but a place lower down the order than it might have been. Nonetheless, Ralf's 2003 championship hopes stayed alive until Hungary, when he put in a drive that had the Williams team grinning from ear to ear. Recovering to finish fourth, after a spin down to 19th in the second corner, passing at will within the no overtaking zone that is the Hungaroring.

In testing for the next race at Monza, though, Ralf's season fell apart in a sizeable accident. He withdrew from the Gran Premio on Saturday morning, claiming that he had a headache – although there were those who insisted that it was a fit of pique after the team asked him to support the title bid of the definitive Williams-style racer, Juan Pablo Montoya.

The team got to know Montoya when he won in Formula 3000 while serving as a Williams test driver. There is great affection for him in Grove. Right from the start, the hard-nosed team was smitten as he arrived at the factory and made a point of finding out exactly who was who on the shop floor, pressing the flesh, making friends. In contrast, the only parts of the Williams factory known to Ralf, it is joked, are the bits between the front door, the lift and Frank's office.

At 16 years of age, Montoya had won the Bogota 6 Hours sportscar race in his native Colombia, at the wheel of a Group C Spice. Three years later, he had followed in so many great South American footsteps to Britain, racing in Formula Vauxhall and then Formula Three. He won the

FIA Formula 3000 title in 1998 and secured a five-year Williams contract – although there was no car for him to race at the time. So Montoya went to America and stunned everyone by winning the CART ChampCar title in his 'rookie' season. In 2000, he won it again, and the Indianapolis 500. Then he returned, as planned, to England and Williams for 2001.

It was never going to be easy to live up to the hype and, in Australia and Malaysia, there was as much incident as speed. Then, in Brazil, Montoya thundered up alongside Schumacher's leading Ferrari and happily traded paint with him as he bustled past without a care in the world.

"Montoya doesn't have any respect for other drivers," Schumacher said afterwards. "Which I didn't when I started! It's great to have such people in Formula One. They put the sport on a higher level." Cynics looking for gritted teeth in the statement were disappointed. In fact, these two are friendly rivals.

Opposite: The young pretender, Renault's Fernando Alonso, joins winner Schumacher, 3rd placed Barrichello and Ross Brawn on the podium at Barcelona in 2003. (Ferrari)

Montoya's capacity for racing is unmatched. Witness his move around the outside of Jarno Trulli at Imola in 2001, at which a bewildered BMW Motorsport boss, Gerhard Berger – no slouch himself – turned to Williams and said: "You can't *do* that!" Yet luck has never been with the Colombian. He scored one win in 2001, at Monza, none in 2002 (even after starting on pole seven times, including the fastest ever lap by a Formula One car with his 161.170mph performance at Monza) and two in 2003.

The fact is that BMW provided the engines by which all others – Ferrari included – were judged, delivering up to 40bhp more than its nearest rivals on a good day. The Bavarian V10s have blown up more often than many would prefer but, in 2002, Williams managed to finish 28 times to Ferrari's 29. The points situation, though, was very different: 221-92 in Ferrari's favour. That clearly asked some big questions about the Williams chassis.

In truth, Williams spent a long time reeling from Adrian Newey's departure in 1997. There was great hope in the carefully nurtured pairing of Geoff Willis and Gavin Fisher

in 2001, but BAR was offering astonishing money to people who knew about Formula One racing cars, and Willis abandoned ship. Unlike Ferrari, set adrift in glorious isolation in Maranello, the busy British talent market has been a thorn in the side of Williams: in such a small community as 'Motorsport Valley', loyalty and stability are increasingly difficult commodities to secure.

When the 2003 Williams came good, it gave both the team's drivers the chance to shine, and in their own way neither disappointed. Both were rather too preoccupied with beating each other though, and all the while Montoya was losing patience with his team-mate's bigger salary and the importance of simply being German within the BMW-powered team. How much the failing negotiations with the team – and his subsequent decision to sign for McLaren for 2005 if not sooner – damaged his year can only be a matter of conjecture.

There was no conjecture about the points that slipped through the Colombian's fingers in 2003 though. In Australia he spun away a certain victory, in Austria his engine blew, in Canada he spun again (and found Ralf Schumacher in front of him to the flag), he made a mess of the whole Hungarian Grand Prix weekend, and went for too conservative a set-up at Monza, when Ferrari threw everything it had at beating him.

Having tossed over 20 points away, Montoya arrived at Indianapolis three points behind the reigning champion with 20 to play for, whereas he could have been champion elect. He left without a hope of taking the 2003 title, after a needless collision with Barrichello resulted in a drive-through penalty, and even more misery was heaped upon him with both a poor tyre choice and a jammed refuelling hose.

Scuderia Ferrari Marlboro embarked on its 2003 campaign in the knowledge that only McLaren-Mercedes and Williams-BMW had the pedigree to take its titles away in the foreseeable future. At the end of the season, though, there was considerable respect for the Renault (neé Benetton) team and its young star Fernando Alonso.

When the mighty new Ferrari F2003-GA swept to victory, as predicted, on its debut in Barcelona, it did so less than six seconds clear of an underpowered, but no less magnificent, Renault R203. At the wheel was a young man who had staked a very credible claim to greatness, the man who many believe will pick up the mantle of the world's greatest racing driver when Michael Schumacher finally sets it down – 21-year-old Fernando Alonso.

Although he was in his hometown, and appearing before the largest, most passionate crowd ever to gather at a Spanish Grand Prix, Alonso made not one mistake. In fact he out-performed Schumacher by quite some margin, most obviously in those traditional Schumacher strongholds of the in- and out-laps that bracket a pit stop.

Here, Alonso was significantly faster, taking great bites out of Schumacher's lead at times when hitherto he had been able to control any race he was in. Although tempered by the youthful impetuosity that saw him destroy his car on the debris of another accident in Brazil, the Spaniard never relented on any corner of any lap throughout the season.

When he won in Hungary – the youngest man ever to win a Grand Prix, beating Bruce McLaren's record by 52 days – it was to head home Räikkönen and Montoya to a podium where the average age was just 24, while Schumacher came home a lap down for the second successive race and the Italian media went berserk with rage.

The indignation towards Ferrari spread like wildfire in the days that followed – for an entirely different reason.

During the Formula One circus's stay in Budapest a Japanese photographer had given some revealing shots to his compatriots at Bridgestone. The magic Michelins introduced to such devastating effect at Monaco appeared, in the pictures, to have worn in such a way that after a few laps they had spread out beyond the 270mm maximum width permitted in the regulations. "We have the proof, because the front tyre contact patch of the Williams is 286mm, 16mm more than what is allowed by the rules," said Bridgestone's Director of Motorsport, Hiroshi Yasukawa.

There is little doubt that had Enzo Ferrari been around, his response would have been swift and brutal – the withdrawal of Scuderia Ferrari from the Formula One World Championship. Enzo wouldn't have hesitated to play the joker that winning a championship without the red cars

was worth nothing to the victor or the sport's promoters, but Jean Todt took a different route.

In the days after Hungary the FIA president Max Mosley and his technical delegate Charlie Whiting paid a visit to Maranello. At the end of the week, they issued a statement to all the teams that the legal width of the tyres would, with immediate effect, be checked both before and after the race – a clarification of the existing rule in truest Mosley style… and pandemonium broke out.

Michelin and its teams threatened to boycott the next race at Monza. Ross Brawn went on the record with a journalist from the *Gazetta dello Sport* and used the word 'illegal' to describe the Michelin tyres – prompting a furious open letter from Michelin boss Pierre Dupasquier, and the threat of legal action against Brawn personally and Ferrari collectively for slander.

Ferrari president Luca di Montezemolo threatened to have every 'suspicious' result thoroughly investigated, which provoked the majority of the world's press into accusing Ferrari of being sore losers. Then, with the hostilities underway, everyone descended on the *Villa Reale* at Monza for a world championship showdown.

The FIA mischievously decided to put Ross Brawn, Patrick Head and Ron Dennis together in Friday's official press conference, and sat back to watch the show. "I think we all get up in the morning and most of us look in the mirror and we know how we feel about ourselves…" said an aggrieved Ron Dennis. "I never have a problem with what's looking back at me. Perhaps other people do, but I don't."

Ross Brawn was having little truck with such jibes, particularly not when Dennis recalled the great bargeboard debate from the 1999 championship showdown. "It is an interesting thing, the bargeboards, in that Ferrari as a company admitted that they asked the FIA for a clarification," he said. "I don't think to this day McLaren have ever admitted that McLaren were the ones who told the FIA about our bargeboards."

Dennis countered with numerous other examples of manoeuvring by teams unnamed to get the FIA to snuff out the advantages of rival teams – or rather his rival team – over the years. "I think all the suggestions of Machiavellian plots is just the normal paranoia that runs in Formula One," countered Brawn.

In contrast with the two implacable foes, Patrick Head relied on a straight defence of the Michelin tyres. "It's exactly the same mould," he said, "comes out of exactly the same mould that appeared in 2001 at Imola." Only when the prospect of retrospective protests against his team was raised did the Williams technical director turn waspish, and he spoke darkly of Formula One becoming "a casino and a charade."

It was a rare chance to see such brilliant minds at work against one another at close quarters, a true measure of the passion that goes into building and racing Formula One cars.

Todt: "We are all in this business to win. If one team is dominant, as Ferrari has been, then the others must be prepared to do *anything* to beat us. On our side we must be focused to do better and make sure it doesn't happen…"

After three weeks of intensive testing, Ferrari's 2003 title challenge was reinvigorated, to the delight of the tifosi and boss Luca di Montezemolo, with Schumacher's inspired 50th win for Ferrari at Monza. (Ferrari)

THE SPYING GAME

Formula One teams shroud their work in secrecy, going to every possible length to conceal the details of their engineering skill from prying eyes. The ever-present paranoia of the engineers was raised to Defcon One when, in 1998, a paper snappily entitled 'Reconstruction of Formula One Engine Instantaneous Speed by Acoustic Emission Data' was published by P. Azzoni and D. Moro of Bologna University, with G. Rizzoni of Ohio State University.

A Formula One V10 fires five times during each crankshaft revolution, so these scientists knew that there were five sound waves to be deciphered anything up to 19,000 times every minute. Recording these waves, and drawing technical conclusions about the engines, was impossible until the advent of Bernie Ecclestone's digital TV revolution. Suddenly perfect images were being beamed at the rate of 100 per second, with the sound in perfect compartments of pitch, tone and time. And the official Formula One timekeeper, TAG-Heuer obligingly added sector-times and lap-times that were accurate to 0.001sec.

Around every circuit, TAG-Heuer erects 19 antennae, into which each Formula One car checks via a transponder. For the digital TV project, the data were fed into a fibre-optic 'superhighway', created to channel the digital TV images between Ecclestone's sinister-looking grey trucks (parked in consecutive number-plate formation) and his mobile 'TV town' – named 'Bakersville' after former Brabham crew chief Eddie Baker, who ran it.

This high-tech set-up made for wonderful TV coverage, the viewers able to tune in to any car. Its side-product was the incidental provision to Rizzoni, Azzoni and Moro of reliable information about the physical progress of each car on each lap of each circuit – and sounds to match. They embarked on a mission to produce information not only on the speeds at which the cars were travelling, but also about engine RPM, gear ratios, braking points and racing lines throughout every 0.001sec of a race weekend.

'Bakersville' was consigned to history in a big shake-up before the 2003 season, however, as Ecclestone abandoned his quest to turn us all on to digital – much to Ferrari's disappointment. "The biggest thing is losing the Ecclestone TV coverage," said Luca Baldisserri of the revised race weekends in 2003. "We used a lot of his digital TV footage, especially the timing. Over the last three years, we had very good timing information coming in real-time from Formula One Management, and this year we miss that. We don't have the timing of everyone, so the race strategy is much more difficult."

The FIA is striving to reduce the secrecy in Formula One. For 2003, it insisted that the teams remove the screens in the pit garages, which blocked out the fans as well as potential spies. It also introduced public monitoring of pit-to-car radio frequencies, although this in itself presented little problem to Baldisserri. "This may mean that we can't speak about the strategy in clear words, but we can always invent a code," he laughed. "For example, 'I think I saw a flower in the truck' could mean 'Come in after two laps.' I don't know… it would be fun!"

There are many other means of industrial espionage available to the teams, should they wish to attempt them. The swanky Paddock Club, for instance, often offers a fine view directly down into the pit-lane that captivates team staff every bit as much as the VIP guests.

"I've seen a [photographic] copy of our engineer's sheet as he was writing it, taken from the floor above," Eddie Jordan said indignantly in 2001. "The whole set-up of the car can be seen."

Successful designers are objects of real desire in the Formula One paddock, and such are sometimes offered wealth beyond the ken of mortal man to bring their talents (and their recent knowledge) to a grateful rival. Should that fail, other methods are available. Teams continue to find members of the opposition hiding in their transporters, or taking 'happy snaps' in the pit-lane, and most likely they always will. The occasional avaricious freelance photographer still tries to poke his camera lens deep into where it is not wanted.

Getting the drop on the rest of the field is, after all, an honourably dishonourable tradition, as old as motorsport itself.

Chapter Ten

HISTORY IS WRITTEN

Reaching the highest level of sporting achievement is not a display of fierce competition, but rather a feat of abject domination. No sport on earth bestows success simply for taking part, and few sports are as hard and as fast as Formula One.

The highest echelons of sport are reached through the dedication of hearts and minds towards one end, harnessing a range of individual skills into the preparation, strategy and execution of success. Few ever fully master the process. So it is that sporting legends such as Real Madrid rule international football, the All Blacks dominate rugby, and the Williams sisters bestride women's tennis.

Neither is sport a showcase for individual virtuosity – although often we choose to think differently. Franz Klammer's sublime talent made him 'Kaiser' of the downhill skiing world for almost a decade, but he was reliant on the skills that designed, built and prepared his equipment, the regime within the Austrian national team that nurtured him, the physios and dieticians who prepared him and the doctors who repaired him.

Motorsport takes complexities of this kind, and grows them exponentially. The function of thousands of components depends on the efficiency of the materials from which they are made, on the design and manufacturing skills of hundreds of specialists, and on the performance of the mechanical, hydraulic or electronic systems that support them, even before the competition starts. Tyre and lubricant technicians make crucial contributions long before the driver

Scuderia Ferrari Marlboro has powered into the record books under Jean Todt's direction. (Sutton)

settles himself into the cockpit. No other sport makes such demands on those who seek to excel.

Since the earliest days of Formula One, only a select few have ever achieved domination. In the century before Scuderia Ferrari Marlboro achieved its modern mastery, only a small pantheon had ever set such a consistent standard of performance that their achievements went beyond victories or titles towards redefining the sport itself.

In any sport, the debate over who has been the greatest is never-ending. There will always be arguments for or against the inclusion of those who have touched greatness but, in motor racing, the very complexity of the sport perhaps allows genuine greatness to be more clearly defined.

The first factor to be considered is the duration of each team's era. Many teams have made a single Formula One season their own but, in such a complex environment, few have been able to maintain a relentless infallibility.

Second, greatness can be defined statistically by the number of races and titles won by the teams during their heydays, relative to those available. These are percentages and they can be misleading, for sometimes it is better to gather points on a consistent basis, rather than to go all-out for glory at every race.

Nevertheless, these factors can give an accurate reading of the achievements of the best teams during a century of motorsport.

Panhard-Levassor – Kings of the Highway 1895-1900

Levassor and mechanic Fournier cross the line in the 1900 Gordon Bennett race. (Ludvigsen Library)

In the Victorian era of city-to-city racing, the dedication of Emile Levassor and the engineers at Panhard turned the first scientific tests of endurance into genuine motor races. Panhard-Levassor annihilated its rivals by proving that internal combustion was the most efficient means of generating motive power, rather than steam or electricity, and that four wheels were better than two, three or six.

From this foundation, Panhard-Levassor led the experiments in performance that began to establish new boundaries so quickly that motorsport soon had to be banished from the open road for the sake of public safety. From that banishment came the beginnings of Grand Prix racing.

Era	1895–1900
Definitive Car	Panhard-Levassor
Definitive Driver	Emile Levassor
Victories	83%
Titles	N/A

Mors – Pride of France 1900-1903

The Mors team moved motor racing into the 20th century. (Ludvigsen Library)

The French motor industry, the most energetic in the world, created a form of no-holds-barred competition that it confidently expected to win. Picking up the baton from Panhard, Mors became the undisputed leader in an age when racing took a phenomenal hold on the popular imagination, stirring national pride in France, Italy and Germany.

Nobody could touch Mors although, in the last city-to-city races. Panhard's ideas were refined and run over a shorter distance where speed was at a premium. Mors invented little but a standard of excellence in its preparation. Conventional in thought, design and execution, the team simply did more things better than anyone else – a lesson that has grown in importance to the present day.

Era	1900–1903
Definitive Car	Type Z
Definitive Driver	Henri Fournier
Victories	75%
Titles	N/A

Fiat – The Chain Gang 1907–1911

Despite the towering engines and sturdy chains to propel them, FIAT drivers like David Bruce-Brown mastered these fearsome machines. (Ludvigsen Library)

The racing fever that gripped the world was inspired, in no small part, by the adoption of national racing colours – an invention by newspaper baron James Gordon Bennett tacked on to the city-to-city races to capitalise on the sabre-rattling of politicians and statesmen. Into the crucible of speed and daring came the simmering discontent between rival empires, and sometimes it drew hysterical reactions from a world teetering on the brink of war, enraptured by the dust and glory of this 'unarmed combat'.

Such passion and drama enraptured the Italian nation, swiftly and unconditionally. Leading the way was Fiat with its huge cars, painted scarlet for Italy. Racing on unpaved

public roads, even though these were closed to other traffic, must have been a challenge in any machine. The 1910 Fiat S76, for example, with its 28-litre airship engine driving its skinny wheels with a chain, gives some idea of the levels of heroism involved in the 'Heroic Era'.

The team's star drivers were Felice Nazzaro and Vincenzo Lancia. Between them they managed to ride the whirlwind of Fiat 's creations and win the 1907 and 1911 Grands Prix and the 1908 Grand Prize in America, as well as taking the Land Speed Record to over 130mph. They set the standards that Italy continues to demand from its racing heroes.

Era	1907–1911
Definitive Car	S76
Definitive Driver	Felice Nazzaro
Victories	75%
Titles	N/A

Peugeot – Triumph of Les Charlatans 1912–1916

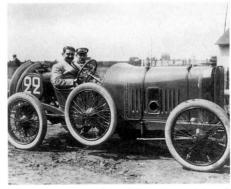

The swashbuckling Peugeot team held motor racing spellbound before WW1. (Ludvigsen Library)

Peugeot – a combustible partnership of design genius and Gallic flair – managed, with no consideration of expense, to introduce such innovations as cylinders in V-formation, multiple valves and twin overhead camshafts to power its small and nimble cars, and four-wheel brakes to control them.

Such was the vision of the technicians under Ernest Henry that it was not until the 1980s that such technology became commonplace on the road. In Georges Boillot, meanwhile, the team had a star driver whose daredevil antics at the wheel enflamed interest in the sport far beyond the technical challenge and national fervour. The Grand Prix hero was created.

Era	1912–1916
Definitive Car	EX5
Definitive Driver	Georges Boillot
Victories	57%
Titles	N/A

Alfa Romeo – World Champions 1924-1925

Antonio Ascari and the Alfa Romeo P2 symbolised excellence in the 1920s. (LAT)

After World War 1 came what is fondly remembered as the 'Golden Age' of motor racing. Italian racing red dominated the 1920s and the concept of streamlining, first introduced by Fiat, was taken further by Vittorio Jano and the 'brown men' of Alfa Romeo (in their immaculate brown overalls).

Alfa Corse conquered all through the mid-1920s, armed with Jano's seminal P2 design and a team of star drivers, to become the first ever World Champions of motor racing. The team brought hitherto unknown levels of strength in depth to overpower the sport.

The standing that its victories gave Italy around the world – still a peasant economy in many ways – was rewarded by the dictator Benito Mussolini, who insisted that Alfa Romeo become the make of choice, leading to a deluge in Alfa's finances at the cost of withdrawing, unbeaten, from motorsport.

Era	1924–1925
Definitive Car	P2
Definitive Driver	Antonio Ascari
Victories	60%
Titles	100%

Bugatti – the Busby Berkley Years 1926-1931

Achille Varzi's Bugatti leads the way at Monaco – a happy hunting ground for the French cars. (LAT)

The success of Ettore Bugatti's bewitching little cars remains one of the most aesthetically pleasing eras of European motor racing, although this was as much due to the economic climate as any great strength on the part of the Type 35.

Through the Great Depression, the Bugatti 35/51 series was the only competitive racing machinery available. Sheer weight of numbers meant that, despite a brief resistance by Robert Benoist and Delage, it was the overpowering presence of Bugatti that defined the jazz era in motorsport, most often in the cultured hands of Monegasque artist at the wheel, Louis Chiron.

Era	1928–1931
Definitive Car	Type 51
Definitive Driver	Louis Chiron
Victories	73%
Titles	N/A

Alfa Corse – *Il Duce's* Ambassadors 1932-1934

Command performers: the works Alfa Romeo teams were the darlings of Il Duce. (Fiat)

Alfa Romeo took back the initiative, its scarlet cars redolent of earlier days of pre-war patriotism and racing under the watchful eye of Benito Mussolini. *Il Duce* feted the victories of Tazio Nuvolari and Achille Varzi at the wheel of Jano's Monza and the P3 Monoposto models, and the French were trounced by the *machismo* and technical achievements of Fascist Italy.

Jano's 8C Monza won both as a Grand Prix car and as a sports tourer, but it will always be the P3 for which the era is remembered. This was the first bespoke single-seat Grand Prix car, which was placed at the disposal of a 'superteam' including the likes of Nuvolari, Varzi, Chiron and Rudolf Caracciola.

The P3's most famous exponents all gathered, from 1933, in the camp of Alfa Romeo's customer operation – Scuderia Ferrari. Led by charismatic former racer Enzo Ferrari, the team prepared to continue Alfa's winning streak. But if Mussolini sowed the wind, he also reaped the whirlwind as Nazi Germany met the scarlet challenge with a mighty silver onslaught.

Era	1932–1933
Definitive Car	P3
Definitive Driver	Tazio Nuvolari
Victories	64%
Titles	100%

Mercedes-Benz – Silver Arrows Supreme 1934-1939

Mercedes-Benz and Auto Union reached astounding levels of Grand Prix performance in the 1930s, and the Nazi government was quick to cash in. (Ludvigsen Library)

"The 1934 Grand Prix formula shall and must be a measuring stick for German knowledge and German ability." So said the newly elected Chancellor of Germany, Adolf Hitler, in 1933... and to that end the legendary 'Silver Arrows' of Mercedes-Benz and Auto Union were unleashed.

Never had motorsport seen such powerful cars: it would be fully half a century before their sheer muscle was eclipsed. Innovations such as the use of light alloys in the construction of engines and chassis, 'special brew' fuels and independent suspension brought a quantum leap forward in engineering. The brutes were handled by over a dozen of the best drivers in the world – Caracciola, Nuvolari and Bernd Rosemeyer chief among them.

Before the 'Silver Arrows' arrived, Grands Prix were at the mercy of Alfa Romeos boasting 215hp and a maximum speed of 140mph. Within three seasons, the German manufacturers could produce 750hp cars that, under a streamlined body, could set speed records of almost 270mph on Hitler's new *autobahnen*.

Era	1934–1939
Definitive Car	W154
Definitive Driver	Rudolf Caracciola
Victories	61%
Titles	60%

Alfa Corse – the Greatest of all Time? 1940–1951

Fangio in the 'Alfetta': an irresistible force in Formula One. (LAT)

The Alfa Romeo 158 was rigorously developed and jealously guarded throughout World War 2 and emerged as the greatest racing car ever known. Pre-war heroes Varzi and Jean-Pierre Wimille prevailed through an Indian summer in the dying embers of the 1940s, winning races redolent of an earlier age before the new Formula One World Championship arrived and, with it, a new star in the form of Juan Manuel Fangio of Argentina.

Work continued on the development of the 'Alfetta' against a determined attack from Enzo Ferrari's fledgling team, and this car took almost 20 seconds off the benchmark lap-time of the 'Silver Arrows' at the flat-out Reims circuit. Although it never had as much power as the big silver cars, advances in handling and driveability brought still greater rewards and the little 1.5-litre Alfetta could get within reach of 200mph. A masterpiece.

Era	1940–1951
Definitive Car	158 Alfetta
Definitive Driver	Juan Manuel Fangio
Victories	85%
Titles	100%

Ferrari – The First Era 1952–53

The foresight of Enzo Ferrari meant that, when Alfa Romeo withdrew, his cars were left with a clear field. The neat and

Cavallino Rampante – Ascari and the stylish Ferrari 500 were untouchable for two full seasons. (LAT)

purposeful Ferrari 500 dominated the 1952–53 seasons of Formula 2 Grand Prix racing and Alberto Ascari achieved total domination (see Chapter 2).

Era	1952–1953
Definitive Car	500
Definitive Driver	Alberto Ascari
Victories	93%
Titles	100%

Mercedes-Benz – Return of the Silberpfeile 1954-55

Mercedes-Benz returned to the fray for a brief, bright spell of domination – every bit as strong as it had been 20 years before. (LAT)

As Formula One proper returned in 1954, a revival was staged by Mercedes-Benz. The former team of the 1930s regrouped without a trace of the political maëlstrom that had characterised its earlier domination. This time Mercedes was racing for its own ends – and it was no less awesome a display.

With the technical muscle of the W196, the time-honoured teamwork of the Mercedes team and the irresistible driver pairing of Juan Manuel Fangio and Stirling Moss, the German marque brought all the strengths of six decades to bear for two seasons of utter domination.

The W196 boasted just over half the power of the last 'Alfetta' but its unsupercharged 2.5-litre engine incorporated desmodronic valves to deliver its limited power to best effect. Within a year, it was capable of over 190mph at Reims. It was to be a last hurrah for the Mercedes *Rennabteilung*, which closed its doors forever at the end of a season marred by the catastrophe of Le Mans and a toll of over 80 lives lost.

Era	1954–1955
Definitive Car	W196
Definitive Driver	Juan Manuel Fangio
Victories	75%
Titles	100%

Cooper's Lean Machines 1959-1960

The light fantastic: Cooper took Formula One away from the grandees and into the hands of ingenious designers. (LAT)

When British specialist engineer John Cooper lashed the responsive four-cylinder Coventry Climax engine to the back of a lightweight, highly adjustable and user-friendly chassis, the results moved Formula One on from its foundations by inverting the grandiose factory team ethic and, in so doing, utterly confounded the racing world on both sides of the Atlantic.

Cooper's reign was short but undeniably sweet. Cornering became the single biggest factor in the sport. His nimble little cars could whip through the apex every time while the bigger front-engined cars relied on being able to power out onto the next straight.

In 1937, Bernd Rosemeyer's 6-litre, 650hp, V16 Auto Union had lapped the epic Nürburgring *Nordschleife* in 9m 46s, bewildering all who saw it. In 1961, the 1.5-litre V8 Cooper of Jack Brabham set a time of 9m 01s. The modern era had arrived.

Era	1959–1960
Definitive Car	T53
Definitive Driver	Jack Brabham
Victories	65%
Titles	100%

Lotus – Superstars 1962-1968

Jim Clark and Team Lotus, icons of a generation. (LAT)

Through Cooper's first breach in the old order came a flood of young, inventive British engineers who refined the minimalist mid-engined formula through the 1960s. The charge was led by Lotus, with the design genius of Colin Chapman and the driving skills of Jim Clark to the fore, starting with the introduction of the monocoque chassis in the 1962 Lotus 25.

Chapman notoriously removed many concessions to reliability in his quest for outright speed, often with a heavy cost. Clark might have won the 1964 World Championship with the Lotus 33 but for its poor unreliability, but he triumphed in 1965. In 1967, the arrival of the Lotus 49, with its Ford Cosworth DFV engine acting as a loadbearing structure, was the zenith of Chapman's minimalism and won the 1968 World Championship in the colours of a corporate sponsor.

Chapman's flawed genius would continue to effervesce erratically, but his achievements of the mid-1960s remain the cornerstones of modern F1 design.

Era	1959–1960
Definitive Car	25
Definitive Driver	Jim Clark
Victories	50%
Titles	43%

The Second Ferrari Era 1975-1977

Lauda's clear vision restored Ferrari to greatness in the 1970s. (LAT)

The youth and vigour of Luca di Montezemolo relieved Enzo Ferrari's faltering grip over his empire. Within just a few months, he brought its chassis construction forward by a decade and, in Niki Lauda, signed up the man who would ascend to the role of the world's most complete racing driver vacated by Jackie Stewart.

Marshalling Ferrari's forces properly for the first time in over two decades, Montezemolo and Lauda simply overpowered the phalanx of British-engineered, Ford-powered cars throughout the mid-1970s (see Chapter 2).

Era	1974–1977
Definitive Car	312T
Definitive Driver	Niki Lauda
Victories	33%
Titles	63%

Williams-Ford – Arrival of the Fittest 1979-82

The feisty Williams team took Formula One by storm. (LAT)

No fuss, no nonsense, and a healthy disrespect for all but their own ends – that was how Williams Grand Prix Engineering arrived in Formula One in the mid-1970s. The rationale has held true through a quarter of a century since.

Frank Williams took three and a half seasons to win a race, then took off into the stratosphere with the redoubtable Alan Jones at the wheel. Patrick Head used the ideas generated by Peter Wright and Colin Chapman at the start of the 'ground-effect' era and built them better than anyone else. Only an abhorrence of 'team orders' got in the way of utter domination that would have been just reward for such a high standard of engineering.

Era	1979–1982
Definitive Car	FW07
Definitive Driver	Alan Jones
Victories	27%
Titles	50%

McLaren-TAG – Getting Technical 1984–1985

The epitome of cool: Alain Prost made speed appear effortless in the McLaren-TAG. (LAT)

At the outset of the 1980s, Ron Dennis and John Barnard reinvented the McLaren team as a high-gloss, high-intensity, high-added-value brand. Dennis secured the funding and technical partnership of TAG while Barnard brought in the carbonfibre materials revolution, and the result was complete domination.

The TAG-Porsche engines in the McLarens relied on sophisticated electronics to manage their mighty performance and, although the early MP4s were simplicity itself by modern standards, they opened the door on the technical age of Formula One.

Era	1984–1985
Definitive Car	MP4/2B
Definitive Driver	Alain Prost
Victories	56%
Titles	100%

Williams-Honda – Reactive Response 1986–1987

The Pandora's Box of technical toys created by McLaren-TAG was ransacked by Patrick Head in his efforts to get Williams back in front. In Honda, the team had a partner capable of greater ingenuity, reliability and power than anyone else in the 'turbo era', and vision enough to

Wild boys – the feuding partnership of Nelson Piquet and Nigel Mansell made for memorable racing. (LAT)

cope with the rigours of Head's development programme.

With 1300bhp on tap, there was power enough to propel the cars at 192mph within the confines of Monaco, all kept firmly in check by such advances as 'active' suspension. Similar engines were used and similar suspension had been developed at Lotus but, with Head's cool eye and the fiery rivalry of Nelson Piquet and Nigel Mansell, Williams produced a 30-race clash of wills that brought 18 victories and more spectacle than any could have wished for.

Era	1986–1987
Definitive Car	FW11B
Definitive Driver	Nelson Piquet
Race Victories	56%
Titles	100%

McLaren-Honda – Simply the Best 1988–1991

Both in terms of the successes it generated and the ferocity of the internal rivalry that dominated it, the McLaren-Honda team will be unique in the annals of world sport. Designer Gordon Murray went back to the ideas he had pursued at Brabham to develop the MP4-4 into the lowest, leanest car around. It presented minimal surface area and, with Honda's V6 turbo, took on board prodigious power. And the drivers? Already a double champion for the team, Alain Prost was the man with whom every driver compared

Ayrton Senna and McLaren-Honda blended passion and technology. (LAT)

Awesome car, awesome driver: Nigel Mansell's ferocious need to win was overpowering. (LAT)

himself, and none more so, nor with such relentless aggression, as his new team mate, Ayrton Senna.

It took until the second race at Imola for war to break out. Senna abandoned a pre-race agreement that the first man into the first corner – in this case Prost – should be left unmolested. The rest of the season was astounding: 15 of the 16 races fell to the two McLarens through a barrage of attempts to drive each other off the road.

In 1989, the 3.5-litre era arrived, but hostilities grew deeper until the drivers finally collided at Suzuka. Prost left to join John Barnard at Ferrari and, while the McLaren-Honda team was never quite at the cutting edge, it gave Senna all the technology he needed to win back-to-back titles in 1990–91.

Era	1988–1991
Definitive Car	MP4/5B
Definitive Driver	Ayrton Senna
Victories	61%
Titles	100%

Williams-Renault – Flawed Perfection 1992-1997

In 1991, Senna was still improving with every race, and Honda was still committed to Formula One, but the sheer weight of its engineering skills created an unstoppable

momentum for the Williams team to go sailing past again.

The FW14 appeared at the start of 1991, brimful of aerodynamic trademarks from Adrian Newey's little wonders for the Leyton House/March team. With the muscle of Williams behind him, Newey quickly became the standout designer of the era.

The 1991 championship was lost to reliability problems, but the 1992 season was dominated by the awesome commitment of Mansell and the mighty FW14B. The FW15 of 1993 was the ultimate in 'gizmology' as Head ransacked every system available. Prost and team mate Damon Hill won 10 races from 15 poles.

From Imola 1994 to Suzuka 1996, the only variable in Williams's performance was Hill. He galvanised the team after Senna's death and put in one of the most admirable seasons in history under the Schumacher barrage of 1994, but followed up with a bigger car advantage in 1995 and a total implosion of confidence.

Only when Schumacher moved to Jean Todt's transitional Ferrari team did Hill finally deliver, this against pressure from new team mate Jacques Villeneuve, who went on to complete the Williams-Renault era in 1997.

Era	1992–1997
Definitive Car	FW14B
Definitive Driver	Nigel Mansell
Victories	56%
Titles	75%

Each of these great Formula One teams shared common components. Some used their all-round competence to prevail by grinding the opposition down on its weaknesses. Others were so far ahead of the field that they could afford critical weaknesses themselves, and still dominate. Such is the game as it is played by the rules laid down in the late 19th century by Panhard-Levassor.

In Formula One design, there must be teamwork creating innovation and reliability, lightness and strength, power and balance – and a benign dictator has always been the key to effective teamwork.

Within these constants, the parameters have narrowed. There cannot foreseeably be another leap of the kind made by Mercedes and Auto Union in the 1930s, by Cooper in the 1950s or by Lotus through the 1960s and 1970s. The difference between a good car and a great car has been reduced from literally minutes to fractions of a second per lap. The concertina effect on design talent and the format of modern Grands Prix conspire to keep even the slowest also-ran within a few miles of the victor at the finish-line.

Minor amendments to aerodynamic configurations, marginal differences in weight distribution, the discovery of a few hundred RPM – all such increments are vital, and many can cost thousands of man-hours and millions of dollars to acquire. Such is the landscape on which the supremacy of Scuderia Ferrari Marlboro was achieved.

Below: Few teams have ever had as much to celebrate as Scuderia Ferrari Marlboro, and few ever will – Suzuka 2003. (Getty Images/ Mark Thompson)

MICHAEL SCHUMACHER: DRIVER RECORDS SET 1996–2003

Most victories in a season	11 (2002)
Most laps led in a season	603 (2002)
Most points scored in a season	144 (2002)
Biggest points margin of victory in a season	67 (2002)
Quickest title victory in a season	140 days, six races remaining (2002)
Most podiums in a season	17 (2002)
Most consecutive podiums finishes	19 (USA 2001– JAP 2002)
Best average of podiums in a season	100% (2002)
Most consecutive points scoring finishes	23 (Hungary 2001– Malaysia 2003)
Most points scored in consecutive races	187 (Hungary 2001– Malaysia 2003)
Longest period leading the championship	897 days (USA 2000–AUS 2003)

MICHAEL SCHUMACHER: FERRARI TEAM RECORDS SET 1996–2003

Most Drivers' World Championships for Ferrari	4 (2000–2003)
Most races for Ferrari	(126)
Most pole positions for Ferrari	(45)
Most fastest laps for Ferrari	(40)
Most victories for Ferrari	(51)
Most points for Ferrari	(657*)

*Docked 78 points from 1997 World Championship after collision with Jacques Villeneuve.

SCUDERIA FERRARI: TEAM RECORDS SET 1996–2003

Most podium finishes in a season	27 (2002)
Most points scored in a season	221 (2002)
Most consecutive podium finishes	53 (MAL 1999– JAP 2002)
Most consecutive points scoring finishes	55 (MAL 1999– MAL 2003)
Most points scored in consecutive races	572 (MAL 1999– MAL 2003)
Closest 1-2 finish	0.011sec (USA 2002)
Most wins in a season	15 (2002, equal with McLaren in 1988)
Most consecutive Manufacturers' World Championships	5 (1999–2003)

Era	1999–2003
Definitive Car	F2002
Definitive Driver	Michael Schumacher
Victories	58%
Titles	90%

Such achievement is made more extraordinary by the circumstances in which it was fulfilled. There was no sweeping, panoramic distance between Ferrari and its rivals, as enjoyed, say, by Alfa Romeo in 1950. In such close company, the pressures have been magnified. The urgency of global corporations and the engineering skill of their race teams have served to turn the screws still further, as has unprecedented public and media scrutiny.

Where does the era of Scuderia Ferrari Marlboro and Michael Schumacher rank in history of Formula One? This is a vexed question, but an answer can be given by comparisons of the great teams in term of the number of races they contested, their percentage of race wins, the championships won and the percentage of championships won. In this way the scale of each team's domination can be objectively gauged.

Overall Most Dominant Teams

	Team	Era	Definitive Car	Definitive Driver
1	Alfa Corse	1940–1951	158 Alfetta	Juan Manuel Fangio
2	McLaren International	1988–1991	MP4/4	Ayrton Senna
3	Scuderia Ferrari Marlboro	1999–2003	F2002	Michael Schumacher
4	Williams GPE	1992–1997	FW14B	Nigel Mansell
5	Scuderia Ferrari	1952–1953	500	Alberto Ascari
6	Mercedes-Benz	1934–1939	W154	Rudolf Caracciola
7	Cooper Car Co	1959–1960	T53	Jack Brabham
8	Mercedes-Benz	1954–1955	W196	Juan Manuel Fangio
9	Team Lotus	1962–1968	25	Jim Clark
10	McLaren International	1984–1985	MP4/2B	Alain Prost
11	Williams GPE	1986–1987	FW11B	Nelson Piquet
12	Scuderia Ferrari	1974–1977	312T	Niki Lauda
13	Williams GPE	1979–1982	FW07	Alan Jones
14	Alfa Corse	1932–1933	P3	Tazio Nuvolari
15	Fiat	1907–1911	S76	Felice Nazzaro
15	Alfa Corse	1924–1925	P2	Antonio Ascari
16	Panhard	1895–1900	Panhard-Levassor	Emile Levassor
17	Bugatti	1928–1931	Type 51	Louis Chiron
18	Mors	1900–1903	Type Z	Henri Fournier
19	Peugeot	1912–1916	EX5	Georges Boillot

For all the science involved, motor racing is an emotive sport. Teams, drivers and cars are treasured in the memory for reasons other than their ratio of starts to wins, or their refinement of the science of hydraulics. None has meant so much to so many as Scuderia Ferrari. In 15 countries, all around the world, the Scuderia's 70 years of Grand Prix racing are celebrated whenever the Formula One circus arrives, turning grandstands scarlet with shirts and caps and flags while the highly motivated staff of the Gestione Sportiva goes about the business of motor racing.

Back in Maranello, surrounded by evidence of the successes that he was hired to achieve a decade before, Jean Todt can reflect momentarily on the record of his Ferrari team. Against such a backdrop, with the 2003 championship still waiting to be won, it might have been difficult for him to name the single most important lesson he has learned since 1993 – but that was not the case.

"The thing that I will think back on is having survived," he said quietly. "You know, if you take my position, one year in the job was average, and two years was starting to be something special. Hopefully, later this summer, I'll celebrate 10 years. I think it's a good result."

And the greatest prize? The final word must go to the architect of this extraordinary Formula One team. Fittingly, it is a tribute to those around him.

"Definitely it is to have built a fantastic team where there is no politic, where everybody has respect for his colleagues from the highest to the lowest level, where nobody is speculating that any colleague might leave, from the drivers to the engineers. For me, that is the best success. That people are really dedicated to Ferrari – that Ferrari gives a lot to them and they give a lot to Ferrari. That is why the success stays. It is the key to success in any normal commercial situation. And it is the key to success in life."

LA PASSIONE

Motorsport is a lifelong vocation. Those who go on to reach the heights of success are somehow compelled to do so, to risk the security that the rest of us take for granted in order to stand a chance of realising the dreams that began early in their lives.

If it is a hard business, with hard people in it, almost all started out in childhood when their spirits were stirred by the sight of a racing car being driven at ten-tenths. For many, the first tang of excitement will always be connected to the scarlet cars of Maranello…

"When I was eight, I used to watch the red cars at Interlagos in Brazil and think: 'Gee, I'd like to drive that one day.'"
Rubens Barrichello, driver, Scuderia Ferrari Marlboro

"I love engineering. As a student, I was also fond of motor racing and, living in this area, the dream of everyone was to join Ferrari. When I had finished my studies, I made applications throughout industry and I received an answer from Ferrari – immediately it was my priority."
Paolo Martinelli, technical director, engines, Scuderia Ferrari Marlboro

"Until I was 10 years old, I always was looking to motorsport as my dream… I'm from Bologna, and my parents came from Imola, so there's a big tradition in my family for motor racing in general, with Ferrari at the forefront. My cousins and I would climb over the fence in the night to see the racing on Sunday."
Luca Baldisserri, chief race engineer, Scuderia Ferrari Marlboro

"My interest started when I was 15 years old. It was the year when Niki Lauda had the famous crash at the Nürburgring. It was clearly a very challenging time, a big fight between James Hunt and Niki Lauda, and that aspect of motor racing – challenging up to the last race – was really fascinating to me."
Aldo Costa, designer, Scuderia Ferrari Marlboro

"I have to say that, the first time I received the bag with all my clothing for the season, it was a really, really emotional time. I remember that day very well, as I do arriving in Melbourne for my first race. It was something really exciting. So it is a dream, it is an honour, it is something very special and I am very lucky. There are not many people who are able to say that they have realised their dream."
Luca Colajanni, Press Manager, Scuderia Ferrari Marlboro

BIBLIOGRAPHY

A-Z of Formula Racing Cars 1945-1990, David Hodges, Bay View Books, 1990
Adriane: My Life with Ayrton Senna, Adriane Galisteu, APA Publishing, 1995
Autosport magazine
Classic Grand Prix Cars, Karl Ludvigsen, Haynes Publishing, 1999
The Death of Ayrton Senna, Richard Williams, Bloomsbury Publishing, 1999
F1 News magazine
F1 Racing magazine
Ferrari: Formula One Team, David Tremayne, Haynes Publishing, 2001
Ferrari: The Fight For Revival, Alan Henry, Haynes Publishing, 1996
Ferrari Turbo, Jonathan Thompson, Osprey, 1982
First Among Champions, David Venables, Haynes Publishing, 2000
Formula 1 1998 Technical Analysis, Giorgio Piola, Giorgio Nada Editore, 1999
Formula 1 Magazine
Formula 2, Gregor Grant, G.T. Foulis & Co., 1953
www.Grandprix.com

The Great Racing Cars and Drivers, Charles Fox, Madison Square Press, 1972
Guinness Book of International Motor Racing, Peter Higham, Guinness, 1995
History of the World's Great Racing Cars, Richard Hough/Michael Frostick, George Allen & Unwin, 1965
Memoirs of Enzo Ferrari's Lieutenant, Franco Gozzi, Giorgio Nada Editore, 2002
Monza 1922-82, Autodromo Nazionale di Monza, 1982
Motor Racing with Mercedes-Benz, George Monkhouse, G.T. Foulis & Co., 1938
Motor Sport magazine
The New Villeneuve, Timothy Collings, Bloomsbury Publishing, 1998
Tazio Nuvolari, Count Lurani, Cassell and Company, 1959
Racing the Silver Arrows, Chris Nixon, Osprey, 1986
The Vanderbilt Cup Race 1936 & 1937, Brock Yates/Smith Hempstone Oliver, Iconografix, 1997
Gilles Villeneuve, Nigel Roebuck, Hazleton Publishing, 1990
Gilles Villeneuve: The Life of the Legendary Racing Driver, Gerald Donalson, MRP, 1989
Who Works in Formula 1 2002, Francois-Michel Gregoire, Who Works Publications, 2002

INDEX